MY SON

(A Journey)

By Francis J.D. Hyland

For my parents, my brother, and my son.

In loving memory of my Grandparents, and Pauline Marzo.

For more information, please visit
www.lulu.com/fjdhyland
www.download.com/isol8

PREFACE

"My Son (A Journey)" is based on a true story. Set in Ghana, England, Zimbabwe, Northern Cyprus, El Salvador and the USA, it follows the lives of Xavier Lewis and his father Albert as they journey through life. It is a fascinating, engrossing and at times a heart-rending tale of discovery.

"My Son (A Journey)" is a tale of a British boy, born and raised in Ghana, and his search for the freedom he believes he has now lost as an adult. As he loses his way along the path of life, he fights with the anger he feels inside towards his parents for taking him away from the utopian existence in which he was raised. As his own son grows, he begins to realize that the freedom had always been there, that he had wasted a great portion of his life in the pursuit of the treasure that he had been unable to see was right in front of him.

(The beautiful front cover photograph of Fort St. Jago was taken by Matt McClure...see http://www.burkinabymatt.com for more wonderful photos!)

Chapter 1: The Dream

Ghana 1975

It was the day after Boxing Day. The weather was good; the season of the harmattan; hot, arid and dusty; the sky a yellowy haze; the air desert dry, a liberation from the muggy humidity of the rainy season. The petrol tank was full. The radiator fluid had been checked. Jodie, Denzil and Xavier, the suitcases and the boys' surfboards were all loaded into the light blue Peugeot 404 Estate – a reliable workhorse of a car that had conveyed the Lewis family throughout Ghana on regular family adventures south from Kumasi to Elmina, Cape Coast, Senya Beraku and Accra on the coast; north-east to Amadzofe, nestled high on a mountainside above the cloud line; north to Mampong in the Northern Hills; and as far afield as Lomé, the capital of Togo. The clutch had been replaced fairly recently, the oil had been changed and so it was with confidence (along with a fair amount of excitement) that Albert stepped into the sturdy French automobile, pulling the heavy door closed with a solid "thunk!" He turned the key and the engine eagerly sprang to life.

"Who wants to go to the beach?" Albert's voice was lively, backed by a broad, satisfied smile.

"I do! I do!" From the back bench seat, the boys squealed animatedly in unison, their arms raised and waving. Jodie was laughing gently, her calm, blue-gray eyes half closed and twinkling enticingly. Her blonde hair was swept forward over her right shoulder covering her collar bone. She was wearing a mid-thigh length, white linen A-line dress that she had had made by a local dressmaker from a design she had found in a recent Laura Ashley catalogue. Her arms were crossed across her lap. Albert leaned over and kissed her cheek, his beard tickling her soft, lightly tanned skin. How he loved this lady! He was drawn for a moment into her soft, alluring gaze, his mind drifting back to the air-conditioned lobby of the Continental Hotel in Accra, ten years earlier, seeing Jodie for the first time with her Gauloise cigarettes and Club beer, waiting for her friend, Mary Bauer (an American professor of Mathematics at the University in Legon), who had taken Jodie's eighteen month old son Denzil to the zoo so that Jodie could squeeze in a visit to the hair salon. Before he had had to leave, Albert learned that she taught music at the Prempeh Girl's College, she was recently divorced from her Ghanaian husband with whom she had had a son – the playful and easy-going Denzil – and that she planned to stay in Ghana, "for the time-being, at least."

"Daddy?" Xavier's little voice snapped Albert's mind to attention.

"Yes?"

"Are we there yet?" A quiet giggle followed.

"Just around this next bend."

Jodie put her arm behind Albert's shoulders, stroking his smooth, black hair. And then they were off.

Albert's head almost hit the roof of the car. "That must have been a boa constrictor," he took a deep breath to calm his frazzled nerves, "or perhaps a fully-grown African python." He was needless to say, a little shaken. Whatever the species, it was huge! Albert hadn't recognized what it was until the car was about to run over it; through the shimmering road haze it had looked like a line in the tarmac itself, a road surface repair, or the shadow of a tall, thin tree. Certainly no creature could have been so long as to stretch across the entire width of the road! With two loud thumps, the car had driven over the reptile. Xavier, jumping up to look out of the rear window, watched as the massive basilisk slithered off apparently unconcerned by the incident into the thick rainforest through which the road had been carved.

"It was a monster. And it's still alive! The monster's still alive!" At seven years old, Xavier was easily excited.

Denzil, four years older than his brother, was watching too.

"It must have been a hundred feet long!"

Albert pushed the clutch in and allowed the car to coast along the road for a while. There were no other vehicles in sight, ahead or behind. Up until the late sixties, this road – the only passage through the rainforest that blanketed the country between the Ashanti region and the coast – had been nothing more than a rut-filled dirt road. The one-hundred and eighty mile journey from Kumasi to the coast road that now took a little over four hours by car had once taken six or seven! Throughout the sixties, the Lebanese had come in droves to Ghana and using their engineering expertise and foreign investments had been responsible for modernizing and improving the road system first designed by the British in the early forties. Albert listened for any new knocks, any unusual noises coming from the car. Everything seemed to be fine.

"We should stop for lunch soon. I'll check that nothing's come loose."

"Not here; the snake'll be angry with us for driving over him!" Denzil glanced behind him once more to make sure the snake wasn't following them. After a quick picnic lunch on the edge of the forest, they continued on their journey. Traffic was surprisingly light as they reached the coast road and they were soon passing through tiny fishing villages – no more than a dozen or so thatched, mud huts tucked away amongst the palm trees, just off the road.

The approach to Elmina was always wonderfully mystical: the surf-misted sunlight; the curtain of palm trees through which one first glimpsed the spectrally-white edifice of the fort; the gloriously refreshing smell of the ocean; it was as though the town were a mirage, a figment of the imagination. From whichever direction one came (one either entered the town from the east or the west), the majestic, red tile roofed, Dutch-built Fort St. Jago, standing alone on a high hilltop, rose up strikingly from the forest that surrounded Elmina on three sides – the small town ran right up to the Atlantic ocean, to a golden curve of palm tree-lined beach with a river estuary that sliced through to a small fishing port. Albert had had a book published on the history of the Colonial forts and castles that lined the Central Region of the coast of Ghana (formerly the Gold Coast, and once a central point in the Trans-Atlantic slave trade) and was well-known throughout Ghana and Europe for his knowledge of Colonial West African Architecture. Seeing the imposing fort (now run as a guest house to which they were headed today), with its seventeenth-century architecture perfectly preserved, perched above Elmina, Albert always felt a stirring inside his body, a warmth spreading outwards as he admired the graceful design. Below the fort, the town – an eclectic mix of old, two and three story colonial buildings, some dating back to the sixteenth and seventeenth centuries, ramshackle huts built from mud or wood, with rusting corrugated iron sheet roofs, and a few very modern, 'out of place' looking buildings (homes of wealthy Ghanaian businessmen) – bustled with life. On the other

11

side of a new concrete bridge, on a rocky, wave-beaten promontory at the mouth of the narrow river that ran between the lagoons and salt marshes and between the busy port and the ocean, built right at the water-line, stood Elmina Castle. Much larger than the Fort St. Jago, Elmina Castle had been one of the primary slave holding prisons and would one day be featured extensively in the epic film portraying the life of a slave castle governor, *Cobra Verde*. (The castle at Cape Coast, a little way to the east, had been the largest and most prominent slave prison along the western coast of Africa, and the site of the infamous 'doorway of no return'.)

The car was welcomed into town by a swarm of half naked, excited young children. Xavier and Denzil held their hands out of the windows to accept the hand pats that the children were offering as they ran alongside the slow moving Peugeot. The fort appeared to be in the sky as the car came around the final bend before the bridge; both Denzil and Xavier gazed in wonder (as they always did), their mouths hanging open, their eyes wide and unblinking at the view laid forth before them. Albert brought the car to a standstill at the foot of the unfeasibly steep hill and revved the engine teasingly. He looked back at the boys, a serious, concerned look on his face. The warm air was filled with the salty ocean spray and the pungent smell of drying fish.

"Do you think we'll be able to make it? I think we can do it."

The boys loved this game; not in the way children love ice cream or kittens or birthday parties, but rather, in the way they adore the thrill of being scared knowing that they are safe from harm, safe under their parent's care; like when they are thrown high up into the air or swung around by the arms. The hill was indeed very steep. The narrow, brick-paved road was edged on one side by a deep concrete gutter and from where they were parked appeared to lead vertically up to the clouds, with the fort as the entryway into the heavens. An old woman, her body wrapped in a beautifully printed, sea-blue and sunflower-yellow piece of material, was sitting on the doorstep of one of the ramshackle wooden huts, a large, white enamel bowl full of soapy water on the ground in front of her, casually watching the Lewis' while she did her laundry. With a lurch, the car leapt into action in a spirited attempt at the ascent. On both sides and behind the car, the children, their skin radiant and beautiful, myriad shades of brown and black, their little faces full of excitement, whooped in delight. Xavier gripped the seat cushion that he was sitting on as tightly as he could; his jaw was set rock-solid, his eyes were wide with terror.

About halfway up, Albert, letting out the accelerator a little way called out gravely, "I don't think we're going to make it!" He revved the engine loudly. He pulled up the handbrake lever. Some children had run up the hill alongside the car and danced around gaily, pointing and smiling, enjoying the drama.

"You two will have to get out and walk; there's too much weight in here." Albert turned to look at the boys. They were pressed as far back into the seat as it allowed, rigid like astronauts during lift-off. Denzil was grinning.

"Come on Nosh, we've got to get out." ('Nosh' was the nickname he had given his brother, derived from 'Dishcloth', a name he had come up with after seeing Xavier regularly helping Kofi, the Lewis' resident housekeeper, with the washing and drying of the dishes.) Seeing that the back occupants were preparing to exit, the children rushed to open the doors for the boys, a multitude of helping hands reaching into the interior of the steeply angled car. After the doors were closed, Albert and Jodie drove on up to the top of the hill where the guesthouse keeper, a friendly-looking, white-haired and bearded man, his skin wrinkled like old leather and as black as coal, was waiting to help them with the luggage. Denzil and Xavier, accompanied by a bevy of laughing children, reached the summit just as large, heavy raindrops began falling. Albert looked up at the sky. The rain was pouring from a solitary, voluminous, dark gray cloud directly above them that was passing languidly across the sun. The harmattan didn't reach as far south as the coast and so although the winter season north of the thick rainforest meant five or six months of drought (and having to endure the fine coat of dust it left everywhere), the south was still susceptible to

14

the wetter, tropical Atlantic weather systems. The guesthouse keeper quickly ushered Albert and Jodie up the steps to the small wooden drawbridge that lay across a modest, stagnant water-filled moat and led them into the fort. The boys remained outside, playing with the other children, clambering over the diminutive cannon that stood watchful over Elmina Castle, in the center of the parking area, running around the perimeter of the fort playing hide and seek as the cooling rain passed.

That night, as Albert gazed up at the white ceiling, bathed in a yellow light from the paraffin lamps in the courtyard below the open bedroom window, through the fine, white mesh mosquito net (hanging from little metal hooks in the ceiling) that was draped over the large, heavy wooden bed, he felt a calmness, a soul-filling contentment sweeping down over him. Jodie was sleeping peacefully beside him; her breathing was in time with the waves breaking on the beach next to the castle. Albert closed his eyes. From the blue-black, moonlit heavens above Elmina, Orion cast a watchful eye over the town.

England 1997

Albert awoke with a start. It continued to rain in the darkness outside. How he missed the croaking choirs of toads serenading one another that one heard constantly in Ghana when it rained! Winter in Durham could be disheartening with the dampness and cold that bore into your bones even when you were indoors. Anticipating the inevitable yawn, he drew a hand up to his oily, aching face. The dream had begun to unsettle him a while back, awakening him at least once each night that it over-ran his subconscious mind, but he still hadn't mentioned it to Jodie.

Lying there, staring into the darkness, playing the dream over in his mind, he saw his son Xavier in that great living room in San Francisco shyly handing the keys to Jodie, dressed as always like a Laura Ashley model. (He loved her from the moment he first met her in Ghana: so elegant, so beautiful.) The dream then moved to the Lake District, to the old stone bed and breakfast with its views of Lake Windemere from the master bedroom and dining room windows.

Albert looked over at Jodie, her face bathed in the soft light from the hallway. San Francisco had offered so much promise, Xavier had written in one of his letters, but now those early days of hope were long gone. Was the recurring image of Xavier, so successful and settled, a subconscious representation of his own unrequited achievements or a glimpse of the future? The dream was bothering him. Why didn't he just get it off his chest and tell Jodie over breakfast? No. It was going to be a busy day for her; Thursdays always were; maybe after supper. With that decided, he drifted back to sleep, listening all the while for the toads serenading their mates in the rain...

Xavier and Katie were staying in one of the front bedrooms; it was their third visit since Jodie and I had moved into the renovated nineteenth century farmhouse. We had spent nothing; everything had been organized for us and arranged so that we could begin operating immediately upon moving in. Even advertisements had been prepaid five years in advance in twelve monthly magazines worldwide, three national newspapers and the local paper, The Cumbria Times. Our closest neighbors – farmers mostly – were a mile and a half away in the small town of Ambleside. Much of this area had been owned by the same families for generations, yet we had been taken in warmly by everyone we had come to know in the last two years.

We spent much of our time organizing walks and scenic excursions for our guests. Our housemaid Irene prepared breakfast for the visitors (Americans mostly, due to the half page advertisements in five American travel magazines) and for us. One couple from Perry, Iowa had come to stay three months ago and were now booked in until mid February. They had planned to travel around England and Wales for six months but so far they had spent one week in London and three months with us in Cumbria. Jodie and I joined them at least twice a week on walks and then for dinner in Ambleside. We would be sorry to see them leave: they had spent two years in Ghana during our time there and we shared fond memories of the country and its people.

With Xavier and Katie visiting, we had enjoyed touring the Lake District, showing them all the places of interest around us that we ourselves enjoyed seeing time and time again. Xavier and Katie had given us a sturdy Mitsubishi jeep that had come in useful on many occasions; snowdrifts and thick mud were common hazards on these narrow country roads. The hefty burgundy jeep had certainly saved us from many a headache.

One morning, the four of us drove up to Carlisle for the January sales. It was a perfect winter's day with clear skies and fresh snow evenly powdered over the fields and roads. Once we arrived in Carlisle, Xavier and I left the ladies to their shopping and found a small café by the river. As we sat down at a table next to the window, Xavier spoke abruptly, as though he'd just solved some complex equation. "Dad, I've never expressed in words just how grateful I am for your influence on my life." He looked down at his teacup for a moment and began picking up sugar crystals that had fallen from his teaspoon with the tip of his index finger, dropping them into his cup once he'd collected a few. "Through your ideals, I've seen the caring, the compassion for Africa you still have, and I know that deep inside me are images of myself as a beggar or fruit seller coming to your door hoping to find you there to tell the housekeeper not to send me away, knowing that you will give me some money so that my family shall eat tonight."

I looked at the tears running down his cheek and gently laid my hand on his forearm. We had grown so close recently; we both knew we had years to catch up on. Outside, below the window, the river Eden flowed steadily heading west towards the freedom of the open sea. Xavier meditatively stirred his tea and gazed at the hills. He had grown into such a strong and handsome young man, much like I remembered myself all those years ago, when I left London for the mysteries of Africa. He had taken on America and had come out on top. His childhood in Ghana had made him so confident anything could be achieved that he had fought for everything he wanted and succeeded. I could see in his eyes that same *joi de vivre* I had felt in Ghana.

After a light lunch at a restaurant on the main street, the four of us drove across the moors, so desolate in winter, to Coniston where my father's ashes had been scattered. We walked slowly, stepping carefully through the snow, our feet crunching through the icy white carpet, a sound like fresh apples being bitten into. The gray stone monolith stood alone, an ancient Saxon sentinel in the wilderness. It was here that I had said my final farewell to my father two years ago.

The sky had darkened considerably and at this elevation, the wind nipped around our exposed faces like a flock of wild darting crows, as though forewarning us of a greater force about to be unleashed. Jodie had had the foresight to bring a warm scarf and woolen hat, both pale lavender, but still she sank into the warmth my arms provided. Xavier set up his camera on the tripod, and with the auto timer on, ran over to join us next to the Saxon pillar that watched over my father.

Evening began to fold over us as we drove home, the four of us still silent. June and Will Lockheart were sitting in front of the stone fireplace in the living room when we got home, shadows weaving about them, their tired faces glowing deep orange. June told us of a phone call they'd had from their son in Des Moines. Apparently there had been a terrible snowstorm that had lasted four days and most of the mid west had been brought to a standstill. We were all thankful for the mild winter we were having.

After the Lockhearts had retired to bed, we took their places by the fire. Closing my eyes, the aroma of the fresh, crackling pine logs carried me gently deep into a luscious mountain forest. Katie brought in four mugs of hot cocoa. While holding the mug to my lips, I gazed into the jumping, spitting flames, the smell of chocolate mingling with the pine. The wind echoed down the chimney like a wailing, lost soul, a sound I remembered frightening me as a child in London during the war. I'd imagine hundreds of ghosts whistling across the rooftops finding a suitable chimney every now and then to swoop down, as a passageway out of the eternal journey of death.

Jodie listened intently as Xavier recounted the wonderful trip he and Katie had taken last September to Honduras to visit our elder son Denzil and his native wife Nina: the fantastic blue peaks of Pukaopalaca (Mayan for Imposing beauty); the real life cowboys with silver pistols on their belts; the vast coffee plantations and the endless pine forests. Denzil had met his wife whilst living in Birmingham and the two of them had flown through courtship, marriage and the move to Nina's hometown of Corquin Copan within eight months.

I put the almost full mug of cocoa, now unpleasantly tepid like airline coffee, on the mahogany table we had brought from Ghana, rose and shuffled to the bay window. I stood for a while, my eyes like beams scanning the darkness beyond the leaded glass. Ambleside twinkled like the first small sparkling Christmas decoration, alone on some gigantic tree. It was as if the Universe was about to be created, the calm of nothingness before the Big Bang. The fire crackled suddenly, the fresh logs burning slowly, the aroma of pine here by the window was mixed with the faint lemon scent of furniture polish on the dark oak plant stand to my left.

The dream ended here. Albert always awoke with those last few sensations vivid in his mind, sometimes so clear he would excitedly check around the bedroom to make sure he and Jodie were really in that farmhouse; and that Xavier really did have a house in San Francisco with that great living room and its fantastic view of the Golden Gate Bridge. But reality quickly sunk in. This was it: this was his life, in this small concrete bungalow and this constant pain.

Chapter 2: Albert Lewis

Albert Scott David Lewis was born in Croydon, London in nineteen thirty-five. His father, an active member of the British Communist Party for many years had died at the ripe old age of ninety-five (still believing). His mother, ten years younger, was still going strong. Two cosmopolitan sisters, both younger and both back in England after worldly travels, lived in the south, two children each.

As an architect, Albert had achieved everything any of his contemporaries could have aspired to achieve. His teaching throughout his seventeen years spent in Ghana, firstly at the University of Legon in Accra, then at the University of Science and Technology in Kumasi had placed him in front of hundreds of students, all eager to learn from a western professor. There were also the independent projects: the Mampong babies' home and guesthouse; the lavish new cathedral in Accra; the proposition and supervision of the renovations to the slave forts and castles on the coast (and the resulting book, which had become a veritable bible for anyone wishing to study Colonial Africa) and other such fulfilling projects that Albert had nailed his name to. Africa had been a vast, mysterious, imposing continent at first, but had soon welcomed him into its great arms willingly, offering a wonderful climate, job satisfaction, upper class living, as well as poisonous snakes, scorpions, malaria and other potentially deadly diseases. Albert still loved Ghana immensely, having found no other country to be as welcoming during his travels throughout Africa: the Ghanaians were by far the most genuinely friendly and caring people he'd ever encountered. He still did work for CEDECOM, the Ghanaian tourism development board, traveling to Ghana twice a year to monitor the renovation work being done on the numerous slave forts and castles that line the coast. This work provided a welcome and much needed supplement to Jodie's income from music and piano teaching.

Since being retired from his post at Newcastle University's Department of Architectural Development Overseas, Albert had sent off copies of his resume to various institutes worldwide, unsuccessfully so far, but he still had periodical work with different cultural societies, UNESCO being one taking an interest in his knowledge of colonial Africa, and there was always the possibility of a permanent residency position in Ghana, at Cape Coast, supervising the work being done on the castle there. Oh, to be back in Ghana, away from the cold winds, the sleet and bitter winters of England. Jodie had expressed her desire to return to the therapeutic warmth of Ghana many times: if only.

Life in Durham in this bungalow, part of Hutchinson farm, although beautifully situated with fields stretching for miles in every direction, the river Wear and a small lake within walking distance, renting this small home on the outskirts of the city had seemed like such a drop in standards for Albert and Jodie. Entering the property market in England in one's late forties was not an easy thing to do, especially coming from a second world country whose currency was practically worthless in Britain in nineteen seventy-eight and essentially having to start from scratch. At one time, one could get two Cedis to the Pound (the currency was then worth about the same as the US dollar), however, when the Lewis' emigrated back to England, renting a quaint old converted mill house near Stone Henge in the tiny village of Heytesbury in Wiltshire, one was lucky to scrape two hundred Cedis to the Pound. This deplorable state of affairs, acerbated by the Ghanaian Government's new law prohibiting travelers from leaving the country with more than two hundred and fifty thousand Cedis, meant that Albert and Jodie had to abandon a good portion of their savings in their bank account and land in England with very little to show for the almost two decades that they had worked in Ghana.

This bungalow was the ninth home in England the Lewis' had moved into, the first one though since the children had grown and flown the nest. Parenthood is a strange thing, pulling you closer to your children year by year and then all of a sudden slapping your cheek as you watch your flesh and blood drift further and further away, ultimately finding a point just beyond your reach. Regular letters from Xavier and Denzil were exciting interludes for Albert and Jodie in the monotonousness of their present situation, a flashback to the incredible life they had once led exploring new worlds and cultures.

Xavier and Katie had left England for Key West, Florida in March, nineteen ninety-two, where they spent two adventure filled years (including surviving Hurricane Andrew, seeing firsthand the absolute destruction it caused – almost the entire city of Homestead, to the south of Miami, razed to the ground – whilst driving through on route to South Beach to celebrate Xavier's twenty-forth birthday two weeks after Andrew had hit) before moving to Kissimmee, still enjoying the tropical weather, hurricanes, mosquitoes and all that Florida had to offer, and were now settled into an apartment in Burlingame, an affluent suburb of San Francisco. Katie was working for United Airlines as a flight attendant and Xavier was an assistant manager of The Sahara, a successful restaurant in town.

Denzil and Nina were living in San Pedro Sula, the second city of Honduras, having spent a year in Nina's hometown of Corquin Copan, and with the aid of an automobile accident settlement they had received in Birmingham, had set up an International Language school. They had also invested some of the money in dairy cattle – as precious as gold in the mountainous regions of Central America.

All in all, one would think, the achievements of the Lewis children would be enough to make any parent proud of their offspring. But the recurring dream Albert kept having had become an enigma to him. Was it a premonition of a possible future? Could Xavier achieve so much? Or maybe it was just the manifestation of inadequacies Albert subconsciously saw in his son. The answer, Albert felt would reveal itself only through self-scrutiny; the idea of which, he did not relish.

Chapter 3: Insecurities

Thursday began as every day did: a cup of tea in bed; Daisy fed and watered (sometimes Albert would glance up as he placed the dish of Whiskers down for Daisy, expecting to see Sheba come skipping in through the cat flap even now, three months after her death); Daisy always eschewing the plate of cat food having the more interesting and alive option of fresh field mice available outside. Since moving from the three story Victorian end-terrace home near the city center to this modern concrete bungalow built adjacent to the old Hutchinson farmhouse, Daisy had discovered her greatest talent (next to furniture and carpet clawing); that of wildlife hunting, and a prolific hunter she had certainly become. Four days earlier, apparently no longer content with the sparrows, starlings, field mice and other like sized creatures that were to be captured in the surrounding fields, she somehow, goodness knows how, managed to kill a fully grown water rat (endangered in England according to a recent study) and drag the dripping, matted carcass the half mile from the river to the bungalow, leaving it hidden in the kitchen behind the larder door!

After setting down Daisy's food, Albert would wash and shave and then prepare breakfast: a glass of orange juice, oatmeal or wheat cereal with low fat milk (except on Tuesdays when soft boiled eggs were on the menu and on Saturdays when fried eggs, bacon and grilled tomatoes were the treat of the week) followed by two slices of whole wheat toast spread thinly with butter and Jodie's homemade orange marmalade or raspberry jam, accompanied by a carafe of freshly ground coffee.

The rain had stopped shortly before Albert awoke and having drawn apart the bedroom curtains, he stood for a while, trance-like almost, somberly scanning the low, dark clouds, listening to the sound of water heating up in the electric kettle. He imagined, for one brief moment, the sky bursting open, spewing like some great volcano, deathly black oil onto Durham city with its Cathedral's towers standing proudly on the hill that was the center of the vista seen from the bungalow's bedroom windows.

During the autumn, the scene laid out before this bedroom window had been inspirational almost. Colors seemed to be changing day by day, the landscape going through some magical metamorphosis. Each morning, shifting hues would dance from tree to tree, discarded leaves no longer necessary in any further designs twitching in the air. The shapes of the trees themselves seemingly transforming as though they were reaching upwards and outwards, stretching at the end of a long, warm summer, preparing to sleep through the winter. The sun also playing an important role, casting varying shadows this way and that way, throwing multicolored shafts of light obliquely down through the branches onto the patchwork of fallen leaves. The whole gradual process had been marvelous to observe. But autumn had long since been driven from the land and for weeks now, Albert had come to this window and looked out at desolation and misery.

The bungalow felt damp. Most of the carpet had dried out without too much shrinkage and could be saved. But the dampness that Albert felt came from the walls. The water pipe that had burst in the attic ran along the top of the wall separating the living room and hallway, and so as a result the majority of escaping water had simply run down the center and both sides of this wall. On entering the bungalow, one could feel a striking coldness, almost eerie were it not for the brightness and homely atmosphere of the place. It was this feeling that struck Albert suddenly, and turning away from the window, he walked to the kitchen.

Jodie looked up as he entered. "Sleep well?"
"Better. I was up once or twice. The rain, I suppose."
Jodie could see the fatigue in his face. The texture of his skin, slightly paler than usual and noticeably rougher than

it had been in the weeks following their return from San Francisco. She saw it too in his eyes, a little bloodshot, but still an attractive sparkling blue. Hearing the clack of the cat flap she looked across the kitchen checking to see if Daisy had found an alternate breakfast; with nothing to present, the haughty cat nonchalantly sauntered over to her plate and began eating. "Don't forget Mr. Wainwright's coming at twelve. And show him the ceiling in the closet." Jodie had finished her breakfast but allowed Albert to begin his before excusing herself from the table.

In winter, the lane leading to Hutchinson farm could be quite treacherous, requiring a few extra minutes for the drive into the city. Jodie had on one occasion, managed to lodge a wheel of the car in a deep, mud-filled rut, bringing the car to an abrupt halt and requiring the help of a tractor from the farm to pull it out. Many years ago, the farm track had been widened and tarmacked, but shoddy workmanship and over usage by heavy farm vehicles had left the lane looking more like a minor thoroughfare in Ghana than a road that was only two miles from the center of an English city.

Once the car was out of sight, Albert returned to the breakfast table with a fresh cup of coffee. He had three and a half hours until the painting contractor was due: the estimate for the repainting of the water-damaged areas shouldn't take longer than an hour to prepare, and then

31

another three hours before Jodie would return from school. There was plenty to do in that time, things that needed to be done: a paper for UNESCO that had to be completed by mid-February on the continuing work being done in Ghana by CEDECOM (progress Albert had recorded during his visit there in September) and also the proposal for a UNESCO sponsored renovation project of James Fort in The Gambia. Both were steadily being worked on, but this morning Albert felt a distraction that denied him the creative urge he needed to write.

Newcastle University had employed Professor Albert S.D. Lewis for fifteen years as Assistant Director of the Department of Architectural Development Overseas, part of their post-graduate Architecture school. Albert's students were from second and third world countries mostly: Egypt, Angola, Algeria, Zambia, South Yemen, Chile – countries that Albert had either visited or done in-depth research on. Jodie had been able to join him on a couple of trips, the two week long visit to Egypt she'd especially enjoyed. (Her Grandfather had been an archeologist there for many years and had recorded the discovery, in the early nineteen hundreds, of the tomb of a young prince at Sakarah. He had spent most of his adult life conducting excavations in Egypt and Palestine.) With Newcastle Polytechnic merging with the University, sharing buildings and staff, downsizing had been necessary: an Assistant Director of an offshoot of the

Architecture Department was no longer required and so Albert and his secretary had been given their termination letters.

It had been a difficult time for Albert and Jodie. The responsibility of being the breadwinner along with her other household duties had made Jodie feel now even more that the world was rising up against her, testing once more her endurance. An attempted overdose six years ago had made the Lewis family stop and examine itself for flaws, problems unseen by husband and sons. At that time, Jodie had been feeling the insecurities, the uncertainty of mid-life living in rented accommodation, the hurt of having one son living away from home and the other showing great disrespect and disregard for authority, education, employment and his elders, something all parents fear most, but subconsciously expect from adolescent children. Luckily that day, Jodie had realized that she had made a mistake and had phoned Albert at the University soon after swallowing the pills and cried for help.

Albert, these days, feared a re-emanation of Jodie's insecurities and had desperately tried to hide this fear since losing his post at the University. Both he and Jodie knew that their present situation wasn't hopeless. Jodie was teaching music two days a week at a private girls' school and also had built up a very successful piano teaching business with over forty pupils at home. Her income covered the household expenses and with the periodical work Albert was doing, certain luxuries were allowed, such as the two-week holiday last year visiting Denzil and Nina in Honduras and Xavier and Katie in San Francisco.

It pained Albert to think that throughout the years spent back in England, they had managed to live with the assumption that should things go wrong here, there would always be a job for him somewhere else, with accommodation provided. The seventeen years in Ghana had been spent living in houses provided by the Universities: lavish, colonial buildings with servant's quarters and large gardens tended by the housekeepers and their families. But now it seemed he and Jodie lived with whatever came their way, waiting for something better to come along. This idea of just getting by, of barely surviving, was the source of much anxiety and Albert knew that Jodie too must be feeling the same trepidation.

Chapter 4: The secret underground bunkers

With the breakfast dishes cleaned up and the sky brightening slightly, Albert left for the river walk, hoping the exercise would clear his head a little, allowing his thoughts to focus on the work at hand. During the summer, he and Jodie had enjoyed many walks along the riverbank watching the schools of trout and minnows that filled this and other waterways all over the North of England, camouflaged in the dark river weeds. The trout had been released from farms that had once supplied the fishmongers of every major town in the area with an abundant supply of fresh fish, but had been put out of business by the larger and more economic farms in Cumbria and Northumberland. The trout were unexpectedly unattractive; as nervous as rats (of that color too) and as swift and devious and silent as rats as they swam for the camouflage that the weeds provided.

There were nettles and tall reeds alongside the path, reeds cleared here and there by fishermen who would spend weeks searching for a prime location, which once discovered, would attract, gradually as word spread, more and more of these hobbyists so that in some areas of the river walk, one would come across long stretches of flattened reeds made even more unattractive by the discarded snack wrappers, cigarette butts and cut lengths of fishing line, litter that Albert and Jodie would on occasion, collect and take home. They both regarded this path as their own private garden and would show no civility to anyone they encountered on their strolls, passing in silence the fishermen seated with their thermos flasks of hot soup or tea, tackle boxes, tins of writhing maggots, and their waste all around them. The colder weather had reduced the number of these 'trespassers' so that during the early days of winter, Albert and Jodie had relished the serenity of nature; the faint smells of hay and manure (sometimes not quite faint enough); the various scents of winter wildflowers: crocus; azaleas; snowdrops; winter aconites, and would listen to the sounds of wildlife and the bubbling of the water running over the rocks and pebbles in the shallower parts of the river.

Large stepping stones had been laid across the river in areas where the riverbed almost reached the surface, making a crossing easy enough for even the most unsteady walker. At its widest point along this stretch, the river was no broader than twenty feet and in some places narrowed to seven or eight feet. Towards these narrower parts, the river walk divided in two, one path following the riverbank, the other leading away, most of the time, to higher ground, as the water would frequently overflow here after heavy rains, completely flooding the riverside path. It was one such fork that today Albert came upon after an hour or so. At most of these forks, Albert had explored both paths on his many hikes, taking all the higher ones on his outward journey and all the lower ones (if passable) on his homeward treks. But today at this one in particular, he could not recall ever having explored the upper path that lead steeply up off to his left. It was close to a crossing point that he often used, there being some disused army supply bunkers in the field on the other side of the river.

These underground concrete bunkers had been abandoned in the Sixties, the army holding on to the land until only recently, a local landowner then snapping it up at auction. Varying development plans for the forty-acre plot had been submitted to the city's planning department, but none so far had met with the approval of Durham's strict planning officers and so the bunkers had been left to decay. The original fencing remained on three sides of the field, the side facing the river having collapsed its foundations, eroded over the years by the rising and falling water levels.

The bunkers were not visible from the river walk and only after clambering up the steep bank did one come across the fallen fence with its rusting 'PRIVATE PROPERTY-TRESPASSERS WILL BE PROSECUTED' signs. These signs, oddly, were facing upwards as though a mighty force, rising silently out of the gentle waters of the river Wear had landed an attack on the secret underground supply bunkers, rushing the perimeter fence, toppling it in one fell swoop, the useless wire mesh and iron poles now lying forgotten and overgrown by the wild grass and weeds. The signs were now home to snails and small crawling bugs.

Even from eye level, once one had walked over the fallen fence, the presence of the bunkers was no more than hinted at. Barely perceptible were dark shadowy areas in the landscape, like little peeping eyes, and long, rectangular bare sand colored strips, all running parallel to the horizon, that disappeared in places behind clumps of trees – small woods that had been planted during the time of large, rambling country estates; a time when a few noble families (the landed gentry) had owned the entire countryside in this region, employing the local peasants as groundsmen, stable-hands and house servants; a time when the noblemen would enjoy their days strolling around their immaculately tended gardens, or hunting pheasants in the woods that had been planted to serve as homes for the wild birds.

With its efficient camouflage, this field had been left virtually undiscovered by other walkers, (on maps too, it appeared non-descript) and it had only been Albert's overly inquisitive nature that had taken him beyond the fallen fence. (Following the war, Albert's mother, appreciating her young son's extraordinarily inquisitive and adventurous nature, had allowed him the freedom to explore the countryside beyond their hometown in suburban Croydon; Albert would pack himself a lunch box and head off, compass and maps in his pockets, on full-day bicycle expeditions, returning after dark, safe and sound, and with exciting tales of his adventures.) Many local farmers erected boundary fences, some more secure than others, with barbed wire and notices threatening a great retaliation against those with a disregard for other's privacy and property. And so, with nothing exciting to be seen from the fallen fence, most of the passing hikers would have returned to the river walk, preferring to discover the mysteries almost every river hides.

It was one warm and hazy afternoon during the summer that Albert had taken the hints the field gave and found, to his surprise, ten identically constructed concrete bunkers, the little peeping eyes were stairways leading down to heavy, rusted iron doors. The rectangular sand colored strips edged by wild grass like a cricket pitch in a small Caribbean town were the roofs of the bunkers. If one stood at the opposite end, facing the stairway, one still had little idea of just exactly what these things were.

With a stomach turning, horror film creak, and a huge effort, the ancient iron door at the foot of one stairway opened and Albert was at once over-whelmed by the dead, musty odor, much like that of a quiet old church only many times more powerful, and he stepped back suddenly, almost falling over the bottom stair, catching just in time, the door frame. Composing himself and prepared for adventure, he slowly entered the darkness, the sunlight casting a long, golden shaft deep into the room, through which clouds of dust, awoken after decades of slumber by Albert's footsteps, swirled seductively.

Scraps of metal, remnants of ammunition boxes perhaps, were scattered about the floor. Pieces of torn tarpaulin lay over piles, two or three feet high, of broken wood. Leaning against the gray walls were a large number of square metal sheets in groups of five or so. Moving carefully so as not to raise too much dust, Albert tentatively picked up one of the metal sheets, recognizing it immediately as a target. The dull orange paint, once bright and luminous maybe, was flaking around the edges and around the few dents, some knocked through by consecutive bullet hits. The black circle in the center was more damaged, peppered with numerous holes. It was one of these 'relics' that Albert had carried home that day and hung on the wall in his study, many times since attaining a deep sense of complete relaxation from staring at it. He had found this target very useful on many occasions as an escape from the pressures of his life.

The secret underground army supply bunkers had become his and he frequently stole away from the bungalow whilst Jodie was teaching at the girl's school, spending hours rummaging around his ten private stores. He had shown them briefly to his wife one day but Jodie had felt nauseous as soon as the putrid smell of gunpowder in the second bunker they'd entered reached her nostrils and she hadn't wished to visit the place again.

Chapter 5: The painting contractor

On their walks together, Albert and Jodie had never ventured further than the crossing point that led to the secret underground army supply bunkers, Jodie tiring slightly after the two miles of uneven ground they had already covered, preferring to retrace her steps knowing that four miles was enough exercise for her aging legs, and so when walking alone, Albert had always gone to his ten private stores.

The path that Albert now stood before, leading steeply up away to the left from the fork at the riverbank was uncharted territory for him. The ground rose quite severely – a good test of shoe tread, especially today after the previous nights' downpour. Striding forward with youthful vigor up the steep path, Albert began his climb. Tall thickets soon obscured the river below and as he continued, Albert noticed thankfully, that the bunkers too were hidden from view on this upper path; from this elevation, they would have been plainly visible. The view though, to either side of the thickets was beautiful: the countryside stretching for miles to the left, woods dotted here and there, and to the right, the magnificent view of Durham city with its ancient castle and Cathedral perched on a hilltop.

His mind was engrossed in schemes to somehow ensure the protection of these thickets, his eyes, like radars, automatically scanning the rough path for safe footing, when SMACK! A low hanging branch caught Albert's forehead and immediately the sharp pain of a blunt incision swept over him, buckling his knees. Falling forward, catching himself with an outstretched hand, the other already pressed to the bleeding wound, he saw the white fog rolling quickly across his field of vision. He heard a long, deep groan coming from somewhere, he couldn't tell where exactly, and then he blacked out.

When he came to, the pain had been numbed a little by the cold, but was still enough to stop him moving for a moment. Opening his eyes, he saw his precious thickets reaching the sky, a mass of slate gray clouds, so low, it appeared, Albert thought he could reach up and tear them apart like fiberglass insulation. He imagined himself, arms outstretched, hands delving into the dark clouds, his fingers breaking through, suddenly feeling the warmth of the sun above, and then frantically ripping and pulling apart the hateful grayness, revealing a deep sapphire sky and the warming golden sun.

A dart of pain shot backward through his head making him flinch. He could taste blood and soil in his mouth. Slowly lifting his head from the damp earth, he collected his saliva and spat. Where his head had been was an oblong patch of darker, blood soaked earth. Touching his left hand to where the pain seemed to be coming from, he felt the warm smoothness he had hoped would not be there. The smell of the river, a smell common to all rivers in England, carried up by a light, cool breeze finally registered in his subconscious, reviving him fully.

A little shaky on his feet, Albert stood for a moment and wiped his face with his handkerchief. Before heading for home, knowing that the wound may need medical attention, Albert looked to see what lay further up the path. No more than twenty feet away was a barbed wire fence beyond which cattle were grazing. It was apparent from the way the path quickly faded close to the fence that many other 'pioneers' had conquered the steep climb before him hoping to find their own hidden paradise only to find a field of cows.

'What a lovely place for a picnic', Albert thought, his mind working to dissemble the pain.

The journey home seemed to last an eternity, each step he took sending a sharp pain shooting through his head. Back at the bungalow, he examined the cut on his forehead. Thankfully, it didn't require a hospital visit and was soon cleansed and bandaged. Albert felt some dizziness, and so sat at his desk to wait for Mr. Wainwright to arrive. It was eleven forty-five.

Mr. Wainwright was a stocky, balding man in his late fifties probably; somehow slightly comical in appearance – much like Albert's father had been. As he walked around the bungalow with his round, pink, shiny head sitting flush on his broad shoulders darting this way and that way like a pigeon, Albert thought his gait, lolloping from side to side and his oddly long arms swinging loosely, made him look like an orangutan.

During one of the infrequent holidays Albert's mother and father had spent with them in Ghana: his parents had attended his wedding in Accra, and again two years later, after Xavier (their first grandchild) had been born, Albert recalled how his father had so enjoyed watching Xavier perform for him. Xavier, a late walker, had taken to giving impromptu performances whenever the Lewis' had company, sometimes dressing up in Albert's clothes, impersonating Groucho Marx, complete with a cigar tube for a prop, or scampering about mimicking the monkeys he had seen at Kumasi zoo. Up until the age of eighteen months, before he discovered the correct use for his legs, Xavier would move around the house – with its wooden and concrete floors throughout – on his belly, using his arms and legs to propel himself forward as though he was

45

swimming (he had learnt to swim by the age of ten months). Xavier would interrupt dinner parties that Albert and Jodie hosted quite often, by sliding into the dining room and under the table, much to the delight of the guests, bringing the dinner to a halt until Jodie had managed to capture the rascal and return him to his crib.

Whenever his parents came on holiday to Ghana (they didn't come too often as Albert's mother was fearful of the "mysterious, dark continent", as she called it), Albert's father would spend hours playing with his grandson, showing little Xavier how to walk like an orangutan or bounce higher on the trampoline the Lewis' had in the garden. The young child loved to show off his lolloping monkey walk and deftness on the trampoline whenever he had the chance. Albert still saw in Xavier the wildness, the freedom of spirit he had as a child growing up in Ghana. In a way, he envied him for it.

"I could start on Saturday if you like." They were standing next to Mr. Wainwright's old yellow van.
Pulling his thoughts together hastily, Albert replied. "That'll be fine. So how much in total?"
"Two fifty. And we'll be cleaned up by four on Monday."
"Wonderful. Thank you again." As Albert watched the yellow van head down the muddy lane, he felt the dizziness returning. He looked at his watch: '1:20pm'.

Albert returned quickly to his study; the past hour was missing and more importantly, he couldn't remember if he'd shown the painting contractor the areas Jodie had specified as the first to be completed. He could call Mr. Wainwright after Jodie had begun her teaching at home; he was more likely to find him in at that time and so wouldn't have to leave a message on his answering machine. Albert sat staring through the framed wedding photograph of Xavier and Katie, one of a set Xavier had sent back along with a video tape of the ceremony and reception with Katie's mother Elizabeth Selleck who had managed to make it over to Kissimmee for the wedding.

Xavier had phoned two weeks before the wedding date, apologizing for the short notice but still hoping Albert and Jodie would be able to make it over to Florida. Work commitments, but mainly the lack of available funds had made the trip impossible. Albert had felt a deep sadness listening to Xavier as he described the wedding and honeymoon plans, and having to sound optimistic to his son about making it over for the event. The idea of getting by, of lasting, of seeing their days out with the assumption that there would always be a post for him somewhere had at that moment angered Albert so much that he'd had to pass the phone to Jodie and shut himself off in the bedroom in tears. What had become of his life? His son, out of reach, about to experience the greatest day of his life and Albert didn't have the money to be there with him.

The photographs that Elizabeth had brought back from her visit to Kissimmee had been put into an album along with other photographs Xavier had sent frequently in letters, an album that was cherished by Albert and Jodie and shown off proudly. Yes, it was indeed pride, Albert realized, that he had felt each time he had shown the pictures to family and friends.

But questions from those who saw the album – questions about what Xavier was doing, the need for details, the scrutiny over his son's emergence into the adult world, a world that Xavier had rejected, preferring to remain in a state of adolescent rebellion up until the good news came, just over a year ago, that he and Katie were finally settled in Burlingame – these 'interrogations' from family especially, had knocked Albert's fanciful views of Xavier's achievements out of focus. Many times he had defended his son's honor, skirting around job names such as 'bus boy' and 'Tee shirt salesman', embellishing and touching up any news as though polishing a used car in an attempt to improve its value.

It was this to-ing and fro-ing between desire, propension and reality that Albert, whenever he thought about Xavier's (and his own) life and present situation, hated having to endure. The dream was becoming a nightmare. He knew that with Jodie's analysis he would be better able to fight the battle his normally realistic and lucid, but recently more audacious, insidious mind had instigated.

Chapter 6: The journey

Albert and Jodie had spent the previous Christmas in San Francisco – one week in a motel that Xavier had booked for them. The motel had been very close to the airport, and so every morning at around five thirty, Albert and Jodie were awakened by the ground-shaking roar of jet engines. They had accepted this arrangement without question; perhaps Xavier and Katie needed their privacy; needed seclusion. The Lewis family had never been an open family; never sharing problems; never openly, frankly discussing situations that befell them, situations requiring detailed analysis, preferring rather to brush them under the carpet, and so Albert and Jodie had quietly tolerated the accommodations provided for them. (Both Denzil and Xavier had been raised believing that a problem should to be dealt with alone: "You made your bed; you sleep in it.")

The two weeks they spent with their sons and daughters-in-law had been a wonderful escape for them both, reviving their sunken spirits. Northern California and Central America both offered mild winters, exciting landscapes and fabulous 'touristy' opportunities. The days had flown by, Christmas passing all too quickly, followed by a week with Denzil and Nina in Honduras and then the arrival back in England coming around prematurely. During their fleeting visit to California however, they had managed to meet up with an old colleague of Albert's from Ghana, Fritz Johansen and his wife for dinner at their beautiful home in the Berkley hills. An envious Albert had absent-mindedly left his camera in the Johansen's living room having spent most of the evening gazing in awe around the fabulous home. The Johansen family had left Ghana two years before the Lewis', moving to Berkley where Fritz had started his own architectural design company, which had become, over the years, extremely successful. Albert had never had the confidence to go it alone, preferring to let other people take the reins. Perhaps, Albert mused, Xavier had inherited this weakness from him, or maybe it wasn't a weakness at all; maybe this lackadaisical attitude was merely a contentment, a satisfaction with the way things were, an absence of greed.

'Foreign from birth'

'There was a child brought up in a town
where the nights were filled with foreign sounds;
African drum beats and the echoes of chains
rattling around the feet of a people in pain.

There was a boy moved to a country where
he felt always so alienated from those there:
an outsider pushed into a world full of hate.
This boy missed so, the place where the world was on his
plate.

He was foreign from birth, always different from those
around him; never quite fitted in I suppose.
 Feeling lost and confused anywhere he moved to,
he tried so hard to find something he could do

right. There was a young man, found a love to care for,
to hold and to cherish like none he'd found before.
She brought his world into reality, showed him his worth.
He realized now that he'd always been foreign from birth.'

Albert put down on his desk the poem Xavier had sent
along with seven others in a letter telling of how four of his
poems about his memories of Ghana were going to be
published soon. Albert had had a few poems published in a
couple of anthologies and literary magazines (he also had a
number of publications about the slave forts and castles in
Ghana and the history of colonial architecture in West
Africa to his name) and so was excited to see his son
continuing on the Lewis' artistic path. However, reading
the poems Xavier had written, he saw the childhood Xavier
had been afforded rise up through the words printed before
him: years without constraints, the lack of an attentive

fatherly hand where detailed in the poems, raising questions in Albert's mind as to how well Xavier actually believed he had been brought up, how poor of a father Xavier felt he had.

Since moving to America, Xavier had found his poetic voice and had gradually been building up a collection of poems inspired by his childhood in Ghana. He was hoping to eventually have a book published, and it seemed that that dream was soon to come to fruition. A book of poems by his son! Upon returning from San Francisco, Albert had told his family this news, excitedly boasting about the positive development in Xavier's life. (As it turned out, Xavier never got around to doing the required work and it was Denzil who became the first Lewis to have a book of poetry published – a book of Love poems in Spanish.)

Before marrying, Jodie's father had written a great many poems, manuscripts that had been kept in the family after his death by Jodie's only surviving relative, her great-aunt. Her grandfather (the archeologist) had had countless papers published detailing his discoveries and on his theories about ancient Egypt. Albert's father was also a writer of poetry and prose, and so with this kind of artistic background, it was a prerequisite that Xavier would become a writer of some kind, published or not.

"I do hope he sends me a copy", Albert's mother said as she reached over, unsteadily placing her china tea-cup back on its saucer.

"He will. As soon as he receives the first copies I'm sure." Albert knew his mother was strong. She had always been a formidable force throughout his life, protecting her three children during the war, sending them out of London into the country, away from the bombings (as many mother's had done); a tall, powerful lady still to this day. "Your mum's like Joan of Arc", Albert's school friends would joke. After Margaret Thatcher came to power, Albert saw in her a closer likeness with identical political views too!

Watching her now, on a two-day post-Christmas visit to his mother's home in Suffolk, Albert could detect a frailty he hadn't expected. Seven months before, on her eighty seventh birthday, she had had her usual vitality, entertaining her guests at a party arranged by her eldest daughter, with tales of her late husband's eccentricities, stories both despondent and uplifting, and generally enjoying herself. Then, so sure-footed and alive, but now appearing to be progressively sinking faster and faster. She would have many years still ahead of her, but it pained Albert to see this decline. Just as he had felt, thirty-five years ago, fresh out of University, eager to make a success of himself and anxious to impress his family, he now felt the same pressures, the stress of having to achieve, but without the comfort of knowing that his education and

54

knowledge would be able to secure him a job anywhere. At sixty, most educational institutions saw him as too close to retirement and as a result he had been offered no second interviews. He realized that time was running out; he didn't want his mother to pass away remembering him as he was now, in this situation of financial insecurity.

Two days after returning to the waterlogged bungalow, Albert had telephoned Xavier and told him of the visit to Suffolk and the condition of his mother, subconsciously hoping that the news would spark in Xavier the same sense of urgency he now felt.

The holiday in San Francisco had certainly been invigorating. So many sights and places of interest had been crammed into the seven days: a trip to the picturesque towns of Carmel and Monterrey (the 'surfing' sea otters had been Jodie's favorite part of the entire holiday); the breathtaking Muir woods (with its towering and majestic Great Redwood trees); the quaint English seaside town feel of Sausilito; Golden Gate bridge (of course); Coit tower; China Town (every sign in every shop window written in Chinese!); the University at Stanford; Fisherman's Wharf (delicious clam chowder served in hollowed out sourdough bread bowls). After the heavy snows and icy winds of winter in Durham, the mild temperatures and sunshine had been heavenly; the sunshine, feeling the warmth penetrating one's whole being, spreading inwards from the skin, along one's veins, into the very marrow of one's bones – much of the aching in her joints that Jodie perpetually suffered from was alleviated within a couple of days of arriving. Albert too had briefly experienced a feeling of emancipation as though a weight had been lifted from his shoulders.

The holiday came five months after Xavier and Katie's wedding. Now that they were married, Xavier could finally begin the process of filing for legal residency and employment authorization with the Immigration and Naturalization Service, as Katie was an American citizen. This was a great relief for Albert and Jodie as their son had spent the last three and a half years evading the INS, working illegally and not being able to leave the country for fear of being turned away when he tried to re-enter, having over-stayed the three months permitted on a visa waiver.

In Key West and Kissimmee, Xavier had found work easily; many small business owners preferring to hire illegal immigrants, young Europeans and Australians mostly, who were more likely to be reliable and harder working than Americans of the same age, and also would work for less money. Xavier had worked in a variety of restaurants, clothing stores and flea markets that lined every major street in Key West and Kissimmee. Walking down Duval Street in Key West on any given day, one would hear a myriad of accents, a rainbow of dialects touting the finest seafood, cheap, refreshing cocktails and various wares.

Katie on the other hand had consistently worked in the airline industry. In Key West she worked as a ticket agent and baggage handler for a small commuter airline; in Kissimmee, for an even smaller, but much more interesting airline started by Richard Branson that flew World War II DC3s down to Fort Lauderdale and Key West, theme flights with the crew all dressed in vintage nineteen forties' uniforms and music from that period piped through the overhead speakers. During a holiday Albert and Jodie had spent in Kissimmee, shortly after Xavier and Katie had moved there from Key West, Katie had managed to get them onboard (for free) for a day trip to Key West. Ghana Airways, in the sixties and seventies, had operated DC3s between Kumasi and Accra, wondrous trips that took one over the vast expanse of rainforest that covers most of central Ghana and then along the endless stretches of golden beaches of the coast.

During the two and a half hour flight to Key West listening to the powerful Pratt and Whitney turbo prop engines, watching at first the flat, dry farmland, and then after an hour or so, the wet, dark green of the Everglades National park passing slowly below the aircraft, Albert and Jodie had both been filled with feelings of euphoria; the

57

awakening of precious memories. Jodie had clasped tightly Albert's hand from the moment the thunderous roar from the engines began until the mighty beasts were silent once the aircraft had parked at the small terminal in Key West. Her face throughout the flight had been alive with excitement, turned to the window for almost the entire journey. The last fifty minutes of the flight was spent flying south west from the Everglades, the antique aircraft following the line of the Florida Keys, hundreds of small coral islands, green and white gems in the crystal clear, sometimes pale turquoise, sometimes emerald green waters of the Atlantic to the left and the slightly darker waters of the Gulf of Mexico to the right. The Keys were linked by one road that led out of Homestead, just south of Miami. From six thousand feet, the islands appeared to have grown around the road like crystals on a string from a 'Grow your own crystals' kit.

Katie had left Florida in February of the following year to begin Flight Attendant training with United Airlines. Richard Branson's DC3 venture had failed and the company had folded a few months earlier and so Katie had looked to the major airlines for work. After training for seven weeks in Chicago, Katie chose San Francisco as her base and had relocated in April. She had always wished to live in California having been born in Santa Monica. Elizabeth Selleck had moved from Durham to California (as part of the 'brain drain' that happened throughout

58

Europe during the sixties) where she met and married Katie's father, a Spanish entrepreneur from Barcelona. The marriage lasted less than two years, and Elizabeth returned to Durham with her twin babies Katie and Alex.

Chapter 7: Christmas

Working for a major airline offered many perks, one being that Katie could give standby tickets (Companion passes) to family and friends that allowed them to travel at a greatly discounted fare, and so Albert and Jodie had flown from London to San Francisco and back in Connoisseur class on both flights for about the same price as a round-trip ticket from Newcastle to London. After the holiday, Albert had seen an advertisement in the Guardian newspaper for United Airline's lower fares for Connoisseur class from London to New York. 'New for 1996: £1,996 return fare.' He had smiled as he read the advertisement. In the past, the Lewis family had always flown in economy class, squeezed into seats designed for people no taller than five foot ten inches, and so their recent journey, seated in reclining armchairs with foot-rests, enjoying the two four course meals with free wine and cocktails had been a wonderful treat for Albert and Jodie.

Three other international flights arrived in San Francisco around the same time as Albert and Jodie's and so the customs area was a surging, turbulent flood of weary travelers glad to be free from the arduous confines of the transoceanic aircraft that they had spent the last eight to twelve hours fidgeting in and out of sleep trapped in.

The fuzzy customs officers, blank faced and bored, waved crowd after crowd past. The freed passengers now becoming anxious as they thought of their loved ones or friends hidden behind the thin plywood partition that was causing a massive bottleneck ahead. From their position in the 'NOTHING TO DECLARE' line, Albert watched the field of bobbing heads in front of him and Jodie, jostling and twitching like grains of wheat in a funnel. The various aromas that floated around the arrivals hall – hundreds of different fading perfumes and colognes; clothing worn for too long; the faint hint of Californian air – these scents, after the twelve hours onboard an airplane were intermingled and magnified in Albert's nostrils to the point of being unpleasant. He sensed the urgency that his fellow travelers surrounding the two of them were beginning to feel as the bottleneck worsened, too many people herded through too hastily. Had they staggered the flight arrivals by only ten or fifteen minutes, Albert thought, much of this problem could have been avoided. It wasn't long though before he and Jodie were just a few feet from the last partition and freedom.

Xavier was waiting amidst another mass of jostling heads facing the crowds exiting the customs hall. It was as though two great armies were locked in battle, the one Albert was part of armed with luggage trolleys piled high and wide with suitcases, boxes and bags that were impossible to control, veering off course and tipping their loads as they caught an innocent ankle here and there. Albert remembered only once or twice ever finding a trolley that had four working wheels. Looking at the 'native' army facing him, so many arms waving wildly, he was reminded of the first four lines of Auden's poem, *As I walked out one evening*. Just as he had begun reciting the second stanza in his mind, Jodie tugged at his arm.

"There's Xavier!" she said excitedly. She pointed her son out, reluctantly releasing the tight grip she'd had on Albert's arm. As Xavier spotted his parents and waved, Jodie, suddenly and completely relieved, waved back.

Jodie had, in the last few years, her self-confidence diminishing as she grew older, become an apprehensive and reluctant traveler. Whilst she and Albert had been sitting at the departure gate in Heathrow, the two of them waiting anxiously for their names to be called (the one disadvantage of traveling on companion passes being that one would only be allocated a seat when all the other passengers had been checked in for the flight), whilst waiting, Jodie had resigned herself to the idea that they wouldn't get on the flight to San Francisco. She'd dejectedly begun planning alternate holiday scenarios, sitting quietly with her arms folded across her lap, her eyes down, leaning gently against Albert.

Even after they'd been seated, much to their surprise, in the comfort of Connoisseur class Jodie still worried about their holiday plans. They had purchased tickets from San Francisco to San Pedro Sula to visit Denzil and Nina, departing seven days after their arrival in San Francisco, tickets that weren't refundable. What if some passengers hadn't checked in yet, she thought; we'd have to get off and we won't see Xavier or Denzil. The mysteries of Northern California did not excite her as it should have and although she slept easily during the twelve-hour flight, she awoke with a tight knot in her stomach.

Now, seeing Xavier, tall, blonde and tanned, with a big smile and waving, Jodie felt a tingle flowing up and down her spine from her lower back to the base of her skull. The excitement overcame her and she surged forward through the annoying crowd dragging Albert's arm, causing the trolley he was pushing to swerve sharply to the left. Reaching her son, Jodie dropped her shoulder bag and embraced him.

It was dark as they headed north from the airport. Albert sat in the front with Xavier, amazed at the amount of traffic there was on the highway. He had never seen a road with as many lanes as this – five in each direction! Xavier handled the rental car expertly, weaving from lane to lane as if he drove on this road every day. Albert had suggested to Xavier a couple of weeks before the holiday that renting a car would make things a lot easier and would probably be cheaper than using public transport and taxis to get around during their stay in Burlingame. In the back seat, Jodie opened her window slightly, closed her eyes and inhaled deeply, filling her lungs with the cool evening air of Northern California.

Albert watched as Xavier calmly negotiated the car through the late rush hour traffic, the orange glow of the overhead streetlight strobing hypnotically through the dim interior of the car. Almost four years earlier, Albert recalled, this scared young man, afraid to face his fears had run from the world he'd destroyed. Xavier and Katie had only known each other for three months before leaving the close-knit community of their families and friends in Durham at the invitation of one of Katie's college friends whom, at the time, was living in Key West. Albert had genuinely hoped that Xavier would gain maturity and a sense of responsibility from the self-reliance he would, with so little preparation, be stepping into. Xavier definitely appeared to have found himself in America, but was still unprepared for the future. Albert's greatest fear was that his son would wind up in middle age with the same uncertainties he now faced.

Exhausted and aching after the full day of traveling (Albert hadn't slept at all during the flight, his mind buzzing with problems he would be facing upon their return to Durham) the apartment that Xavier and Katie were renting could have been a garage for all he cared as he and Jodie sat down together on the bright red sofa. Albert glanced around the room noticing that none of the lovely furniture Xavier and Katie had had in Kissimmee was here. Everything they had accumulated during their three and a half years in Florida had been sold, the cost of shipping it across the country being too great.

It was just as Albert was about to ask Xavier to help him carry the suitcases in from the car that Xavier broke the news. "Mum and Dad, Katie and I have booked a motel for you. We've already paid for it. We thought you'd be more comfortable in a real bed than on this sofa bed."

At the mention of a motel, Albert's mind conjured up various images of the wonderful places they'd stayed at in Ghana: exotic beach-front chalets, graceful colonial buildings in Accra and the impeccably restored Portuguese Catholic Mission in Asamakese.

"Most places were fully booked," Xavier continued, clearly nervous about something. It was two days before Christmas and so it was entirely feasible that this statement was true, but as they drove through the adjoining town of San Mateo, passing many hotels and motels, each progressively paltrier the further they drove, Albert turned to look at Xavier.

"Wasn't there anything closer?" he asked sullenly.

"There were two places about a mile back, but the rooms were awfully dirty and smelly. We're here now. This is the place, up on the left."

Xavier pulled into the forecourt of The Knight's Inn Motel; it had none of the appeal that Albert's images of the places in Ghana had. He asked himself how much a place like this could charge. The greatest cause of disappointment, Albert reminded himself, was having too high expectations of anyone or any situation. The room Xavier left them in was nice enough, Jodie reasoned, and so Albert relinquished the idea of finding some other accommodation the next day. Feeling the effects of the arduous journey, they hastily unpacked and were both promptly sound asleep.

The resting ended at five thirty in the morning as the window shook noisily, the first of the many airplanes headed for the East Coast. Every fifteen minutes or so, the motel room would vibrate as another plane flew directly over-head. Xavier arrived at nine to take his parents for breakfast. As soon as Albert had opened the door and greeted his son with a hug and a faint kiss on the cheek,

Xavier noticed the almost complete absence of vivacity that he had expected to see in his father. He sat down in silence on the end of the unmade bed, puzzled as to what could have subdued his father's enthusiasm. Albert rustled through the motel's colorful Visitor's Guide in one of the two uncomfortable-looking armchairs by the window; the heavy curtains drawn open slightly allowing bright sunlight to stream in to the gloominess of the room setting him in silhouette. While the two pensive men waited for Jodie to finish applying her make-up, another plane passed over the motel. "What time did that start?"

"About two hours ago. We were already up though," Albert fibbed, glancing nervously at Jodie who was fortunately out of earshot; Albert knew that even if she'd been a little closer her tinnitus would have most likely blurred the conversation anyway.

The road into Burlingame, after passing the city limit sign, 'Pop. 27,205', Albert managed to read, was lined with majestic eucalyptus trees, their rough, gray bark shedding in places to reveal smooth, silken swirls of pale orange, brown, ash and cream. The fresh warm air was thick with their delectable perfume; Albert breathed in deeply and smiled.

The time passed quickly and before Albert had a chance to reflect on the sightseeing done since breakfast, they had met Katie at the airport and were back at the apartment.

Jodie was particularly pleased to greet her new daughter-in-law and she and Katie sat and talked throughout the late lunch Xavier had prepared. Albert listened to their incessant conversation as he ate, watching the two ladies enjoying a good old gossip.

Since Elizabeth Selleck had returned from Kissimmee and delivered the wedding photographs and video, they had developed a close friendship, the three of them often enjoying Sunday lunches and walks together. Jodie and Elizabeth would share the latest news from their children, letters, postcards and phone-calls from America. Elizabeth had traveled across Canada before settling in California in the sixties leaving, as Albert and Jodie had done, the depression of England for a more fulfilling life. She had worked at University Hospital in San Francisco and lived in the infamous Haight-Ashbury district for a number of years. Before they left for their holiday, Elizabeth had given Albert and Jodie a list of places she felt were well worth visiting.

The sights and sounds (early morning airplanes aside), the smells and most importantly for Jodie, the warm weather that Albert and Jodie experienced during their brief but none-the-less exhilarating holiday in San Francisco combined with the joy of seeing their youngest son happily married, lifted the Lewis' spirits and sent them onward to Honduras for further warming and spirit lifting preparing them for their rude homecoming.

Chapter 8: Analysis

Albert heard the car approaching. He looked at his watch: 3:20pm. She's late, he thought. Joseph, her first pupil would be here in five or ten minutes. Albert hurriedly filled the kettle, turned it on and put two tea bags in the teapot. "How was school?" He kissed her as she came through the door.

"It was okay. The lane's terrible though. What's the plaster for?" She touched Albert's forehead near the wound, concern obvious in her expression, and moved her head back slightly to wait for his explanation.

"It's just a graze. I was walking by the river and a branch caught me".

Jodie frowned doubtingly. "Mr. Wainwright's going to start on Saturday. He said everything would be finished by Monday afternoon," Albert said as he walked back into the kitchen to prepare the tea. Jodie followed him, still carrying her shoulder bag. She removed her coat, laid it over a chair and sat down at the kitchen table.

"Where did it happen?" she asked, still concerned about her husband's injury.

"Near the army field. I didn't see the branch, it was a path I hadn't been along before." He put down a cup of tea in front of Jodie. "Really, it's nothing. Don't worry."

"Did you show Mr. Wainwright the closet?"

Albert looked down at his tea, his mind racing. "Yes. You'd better get ready darling, Joseph will be here any minute." Albert watched his wife as she picked up her cup of tea and left the room. The doorbell rang as soon as she had disappeared. Albert heard Jodie welcoming her piano pupil in and sat down in the seat Jodie had just left and heaved a sigh of relief.

The scales began in the next room as Albert stood up and went to the phone on the wall by the larder and dialed Mr. Wainwright's number. "Hello, this is Ted Wainwright."

"Oh, hello Mr. Wainwright, it's Albert Lewis. How are you?"

"Fine. How can I help you Mr. Lewis?"

"One question, did you include the closet and hallway in your estimate?"

"Yep. Two fifty, right?"

"That's fine. And could you do the hallway first?" Albert still could not recall any part of Mr. Wainwright's visit.

"That's what we arranged, isn't it. Then the room with the piano." After hanging up the phone, Albert poured himself another cup of tea. The rain had started again, falling from the slate gray sky.

During supper, Albert had finally recounted his recurring dream to Jodie. She listened intently, ignoring her plate as Albert spoke. "Why didn't you tell me about it before?" Jodie was watching Albert carefully.

"I don't know. I suppose I hoped that it would stop happening." Albert looked up at Jodie searchingly. She was quiet for a moment as she sipped her wine.

"Xavier doesn't know where he's going. Look at Denzil; he's thirty-one and still trying to find out what's best for him. I think that nowadays you've just got to take whatever you can."

Denzil was Jodie's son to her first husband, a Ghanaian she'd met whilst at University in London, a son Albert had accepted willingly as his own when he married Jodie. Even after Xavier had been born, Albert had shown neither one any more love or favoritism. Albert had paid for Denzil to attend one of the best private schools in England, Bembridge School on the Isle of Wight; a boarding school that Denzil began attending when he was eleven years old. Denzil had excelled at athletics during his six years at Bembridge, breaking school records in the one and two hundred meter sprints, the shot-putt, discus, and long jump. After leaving school without any academic qualifications, Denzil had spent five or six years searching for a goal. The Police Force had inspired him for a number of years, but he had willingly resigned and moved to Honduras with his new wife, hoping to find a more fulfilling existence.

Jodie left the table and went over to the sofa. "We can't expect more from our children than what's available to them. I mean, look at the CDs that Xavier has made. Just because he's not an architect, you can't worry for him. I know you think that he believes that music will be his future. There's nothing wrong with that. And what about his poems?"

Albert pushed his plate away and sat back, folding his arms. "I don't know why I keep having this dream. I'm aware of what Xavier has done, but..." He sighed, turning his head to look at Jodie. "I don't think he's responsible enough for marriage. He's got Katie to think about now."

"He's nearly twenty-eight Albert! He's old enough to know what he's doing and what needs to be done."

Jodie lit up a Gauloise and settled into the sofa. Albert saw the raised vein on her neck. The smoke from the cigarette rose vertically for three or four feet in an almost perfectly straight line, dissipating just below the ceiling creating the illusion that the cigarette was being suspended from the ceiling by a fine silk thread. "He just needs to find the right direction in which to go. He's very intelligent. Once he applies himself he'll be able to do anything, and do it well." Frowning, Jodie tapped the ash from the tip of the French cigarette and looked over at Albert, still seated at the dining table. "He's kept himself out of trouble. You know how fast he was slipping before he left." Jodie

73

remembered vividly how Xavier's increasingly delinquent behavior throughout the year before he met Katie had affected Albert, and hoped that what she'd just said wouldn't instigate another heated discussion about Xavier's "fall from grace", as Albert had once put it, but rather instill in her husband's mind some optimism for their son's future.

"I suppose you're right. In that respect he's done well." Albert watched as Jodie inhaled and then, her lips pouting, blew a puff of smoke upwards. He stood up and went into the kitchen.

A tingle swept across the surface of Albert's skin as he recalled the first time he'd seen Jodie. He'd been waiting in the lobby of the Continental Hotel in Accra for Bob Barker, a visiting lecturer from University College in London, the college Albert had studied at. Jodie, her long golden blonde hair swept forward over her shoulder, had been sitting in one of the leather armchairs opposite him, with a bottle of Club beer on the low wicker table that separated them, smoking a Gauloise cigarette and reading a book by the local author R.E. Obeng. The scene could have been a photograph in a fashion magazine, Albert remembered thinking.

Having lived as a bachelor in Accra for the past five years, Albert had always kept an eye out for female companions. He had introduced himself to Jodie and the two of them talked about London and teaching in Africa until Bob Barker appeared. Departing, Albert had turned and seen Jodie, her lips pouting as though blowing a kiss, exhale a puff of smoke into the cool air of the hotel's lobby; they had exchanged fleeting smiles, and then he and the visiting lecturer were out in the sweltering heat of the tropics and off to the University of Legon.

"Remember how he withdrew after we moved to Durham?" Jodie remarked as Albert re-entered the room. "I think he must have hated us for taking him away from Ghana." Jodie was speaking softly, her eyes squinting and with a distance in them that Albert hadn't seen before. "He spent what, five or six years in his own world," she continued.

"That was adolescence surely! Every child goes through a period like that."

Albert brought over two mugs of milky coffee and handed one to Jodie. "They do, but they still make friends at school. Xavier pulled himself away completely."

"He was bullied. Withdrawing was purely a reaction to that" Albert tried to reason.

"No, I think it was more serious than that. Even once he started those bodybuilding competitions, he was more confident, but he still didn't integrate." This was true, Albert remembered. He pictured Xavier showing off to his family after Sunday lunches, going through the posing routines he used on stage at the regional bodybuilding contests, his young, bright blue eyes alight with pride and self-confidence.

"So you think us moving to England angered Xavier to such a great extent that he hated us for it?" Albert was unsettled by this possibility.

"I'm sure it was upsetting for him, being taken away from the carefree life he had in Ghana, and at that age, he wouldn't have understood fully why. He could well have blamed us for it."

"But what was wrong with the life he had here?" Albert swirled the coffee around in the mug to stop the milk from coagulating.

"He never has viewed England as his home. You saw the Ghana flag in the apartment in Burlingame. He was brought up with Ghanaian and Lebanese and Scandinavian children; I'm sure he couldn't relate to the children here, especially those here in Durham. You're forgetting how closed-minded some people are here." Jodie was on the defensive again.

"No I'm not!" Albert retorted. "I don't see how our life was any worse than it was in Ghana towards the end."

"That's just it: you don't see how 'our life' was any worse. You have to look at it from Xavier's point of view!" With this, Jodie stood up, her knees cracking as she straightened, and walked out of the room. Albert's eyes followed her for a second or two and then he looked down at his mug of coffee and inhaled deeply. The sweet aroma of French tobacco lingered in the air. He reached for the mug, Jodie's last words playing over in his mind. He had never thought of himself as being, to any degree, self-centered. On the contrary, he saw himself as having lived his life helping others, always giving more than he ever received, unbegrudgingly and willingly. How could Jodie accuse him of not considering Xavier's feelings? He now felt more confused than before.

Suddenly, Jodie appeared in the doorway to the kitchen and walked over to him. She clasped Albert's hands in hers. "I'm sorry darling. We didn't do anything wrong in the way we raised Xavier; he's just spoilt. I mean, who wouldn't be, having a childhood like that? Leaving Ghana was necessary. He can see that now, I'm sure. Let's wash up and go off to bed." Jodie kissed him and began clearing the table.

Chapter 9: Stolen

The sky was wonderfully clear. Albert gazed at the new colors outside as he ate his breakfast. He knew from past experience that the fine weather wouldn't last more than a day or two. "How do you fancy a picnic lunch dear?"

Jodie, about to eat a spoonful of cereal, paused for a moment as she turned to look at Albert. "I'm sure it's still very cold out there and the forecast said it might rain later on."

"Well, we could make a few sandwiches and if it does then we'll have them indoors. But I think it's going to be fine all day. What do you say?"

"Where were you thinking of going to?"

"Funnily enough, by the trees where I bumped my head. You get a lovely view of the countryside and the cathedral from up there." Albert could still feel a dull pain in his forehead. He ignored it and the morning continued, the fair weather fighting the bleak winter.

They sat away from the shade of the oak trees, the weak January sun warming their scalps enough to feel comfortable. "Is this the place?" Jodie had inquired obviously unimpressed after reaching the top of the steep bank. Albert humbly gazed out across the countryside, absorbing the tranquility as he ate a ham and cheese sandwich. The ground, through the thin raffia mat was cold, but bearable. After forty minutes or so with little conversation, Jodie began tidying up the picnic things. Some snowdrops were growing close to where they were sitting. Albert reached over to pick one and tenderly handed it to his wife. "Things are going to be fine," he said as he leaned across and kissed Jodie's cheek. They cleared up the remnants of the picnic lunch and set off for home, hand in hand along the river walk, the sun, high in the clear blue sky, warming the backs of their heads and shoulders. "We'd better start preparing the house for Mr. Wainwright", Albert said as they neared the bungalow. "He'll be here tomorrow morning."

"What time did he say he'd start?"

"Well, I'm not sure exactly what time he said he'd be here, but we'd better have everything ready first thing so that he can keep to his schedule."

The rain didn't start until after Jodie's first pupil had arrived. Albert sat in the kitchen watching the raindrops combine with one another and run down the window, listening to the scales repeated over and over in the next room. "Everything IS going to be fine!" he stated emphatically to himself as he looked at the still erect snowdrop Jodie had placed in a glass on the kitchen table.

Albert thought about lighting a fire but then remembered that the cover had been blown off the woodpile a couple of nights ago. Instead, he set about preparing supper.

"Oh God, No!" The words slid from Albert's lips like molten lead, his breath steaming in the cold Sunday morning air. He started at the space in which, an hour and a half earlier, he'd carefully reversed the car into. His mouth gaped like a child's at the circus.

"Have you forgotten where you parked it Albert?" Tom Stoddart chuckled as he and his wife crossed the road nearby.

"I think it's been stolen," Albert replied, knowing he wasn't that senile yet.

The Stoddarts watched as Albert walked up and down the street opposite the church.

"You should call the Police right away Albert, it may just have happened. Come on, we'll find a phone box and then I'll run you home."

"Thanks Tom." Albert was still trying to comprehend the situation. "What would anyone want with an old car like that?"

"The old ones are probably easier to get into," Tom suggested.

The car was found later that day in a rundown housing estate on the north side of Newcastle. It was a write-off: all the windows had been smashed, the dashboard had been ripped apart and parts had been stripped off the engine. Joyriding was a major problem at that time in the North of England, the Police seemingly at a loss as to how to control it.

"What are we going to do now" Jodie asked rhetorically after the Police had called with the news. "We can't walk into town everyday with the weather the way it's been."

"We'll manage darling," Albert said as he hugged his distraught wife. 'Why us Lord?' Albert prayed as he held her. He could feel Jodie shaking and for a brief moment, thought that she was laughing. He bit his lower lip to stop himself from showing his own pain.

Lunch had been a horribly somber affair, and now, as he made a pot of tea, Albert felt another weight settling down on his shoulders. He stood by the sink, his hands grasping the countertop and stared vacantly out through the window. The owner of the neighboring farm had moved a hundred or so sheep that day into the field opposite the bungalow. The lazy creatures were mostly sitting, bored and cold, but there were a few standing grazing or staring blankly ahead.

"Aren't they funny?" Jodie said from behind, startling Albert. He turned to face her.

"What darling?"

"The sheep. They're probably wondering why they've been moved here. They look like they're lost." Jodie put her arms around her husband and pulled herself close.

"What time is will it be in San Francisco? Let's call Xavier." Jodie rested her chin on Albert's shoulder.

Xavier's light heart and the news that his application for permanent residency had been conditionally approved made both Albert and Jodie feel a lot happier. The precariousness of Xavier's situation over the years had been of great concern to Albert especially; the embarrassment of having his son deported from America as an illegal alien would have been awful. He often thought back to the times he'd had to word his answers carefully as family and friends questioned him about Xavier's life in Durham, at first having to make sure they hadn't heard any stories from other sources. A local newspaper had once reported, in a quarter page article, the details of one of Xavier's court appearances, with a large photograph, ironically, of Xavier and another model advertising some jewelry store on the opposite page.

Chapter 10: Reflection

Xavier's birth was a wonderful celebration of life for Albert, then in his mid-thirties. He called his parents in England within a couple of hours to break the good news. He and Jodie hadn't decided on a name for the new baby, and so as it was Palm Sunday, Albert's two sisters, at home with their parents for the Easter Holiday, had named him Hosannah, a name they and Albert's mother used until they finally met the infant eight months later when Albert, Jodie and Denzil traveled to England for Christmas. At home, he was called Kwesi X – Kwesi being the Ashanti name given to Sunday born males.

Albert's parents, on hearing of Jodie's pregnancy and not trusting the quality of any medical facilities outside of England, suggested to their son that the baby should be born in England. Albert reassured them that everything would be fine and that an Irish doctor would be taking care of Jodie during her pregnancy and delivering the baby.

Denzil took to Xavier immediately, enjoying having a baby brother to show off to. Never rough, he played with Xavier for hours on end, attempting to pass on to the infant all the wisdom he had accumulated in his four years. Denzil went through sheets and sheets of drawing paper showing off his artistic and calligraphic skills to baby Xavier who would sit quietly watching and listening intently as his older brother attempted to educate him. The two nannies that looked after the Lewis children also absolutely adored the chubby, pink infant with white hair. They would take turns in parading him around the village, strapped, in the local fashion, to their backs with bright, colorful hand-woven kenti cloth.

Xavier was fortunate too for having Baby Kofi to grow up with. Born three weeks after Xavier, Baby Kofi was the forth child to the Lewis' resident housekeeper Kofi Amamu and his wife. Kofi, a tall, handsome, well-built man, lived with his family in a small and very basic house at the back of the Lewis' property. Every member of staff at the University of Science and Technology in Kumasi was provided with accommodations; large colonial style buildings with large gardens and servants' quarters. The 'servants' (as the expatriates who had been in Ghana since before Independence called them), usually recommended to the newly arrived expatriates by fellow staff members, were paid reasonably well (by local standards) and were responsible for, among other things, house cleaning,

84

cooking, washing the dishes, laundry and ironing, tending the garden – which in the Lewis' case contained a wonderful array of fruit bearing plants: mango; orange; grapefruit; paw-paw; sour-sop; avocado pear; pineapple; banana; fruit that Kofi would keep the Lewis (and his own) family pleasured with. During its fruiting season, the towering mango tree, with its great shade canopy, was ransacked daily by the children who, for hours after would be left with their hands stained orange, bright orange rings around their lips and mango fur stuck in between their front teeth. In the fenced yard surrounding his house, Kofi grew a number of fruits and vegetables and kept a variety of 'pets'. There were, at any given time, half a dozen hens, a cockerel, three or four guinea fowl and a couple of goats. With the help of his family, he maintained his small 'farm' and was pretty much self-sufficient. The chickens were usually escapees from the poultry farm that one of the Lewis' neighbors, a colleague of Albert's at UST, operated in his back garden.

This poultry farm conveniently provided many a fine Sunday lunch for the Lewis'. Kofi would pick out a succulent looking chicken, carry it home by its wings, and with all the children looking on in awe, slit the poor thing's throat, drain the blood into a small hole he'd dug in the ground and then finally decapitate the desperately struggling creature. Kofi would then let go of the headless bird and the children would chase after it excitedly as it ran, helter skelter around the garden for a minute or so before collapsing in the grass. Drawn outside by the cacophony raised by the alarmed animals in Kofi's yard and the children whooping wildly, Albert and Jodie would stand and watch in amusement, the children darting to and fro behind the bird.

The Lewis' house, in the small village of Nhyaesu, (pronounced "Nin-cha-su"), just outside Kumasi was like many others around it. The University owned many properties in the village in which it housed its (mostly foreign) professors. The Lewis' neighbors were from all over the world: Canada; The Lebanon; Syria; Holland; Germany; America; Iran; Nigeria: most of them with children who attended the nearby Ridge school. Dinner parties, very common amongst the expatriate community in Nhyaesu, were fabulous affairs: the cultural diversity; the various ethnic and European cuisines that the Lewis family was exposed to made for an extremely interesting life, especially for the Lewis boys as they grew up. The neighborhood was a safe, comfortable and friendly place to live. Even the residents of the shantytown at the end of the street that the Lewis' lived on seemed to be content living their impoverished lives, and coexisted peacefully in a strange kind of equilibrium with their affluent foreign neighbors.

The families from the shantytown – living in tiny huts made from mud, wood or sheets of rusted corrugated iron; the street edged by concrete gutters that were lined with a filthy white scum, as thick and white as the skin on boiled milk, the fluids beneath heated and churned by the afternoon sun, giving off a piercing, acrid smell that on steamy, breezeless days could be almost suffocating – the families who lived in this squalor survived by growing fruits and vegetables on carefully tended plots of earth behind their huts. What they didn't use for their own families, they would either sell by the roadside or at the huge market in Kumasi or they would (as was the most lucrative method), by befriending the expatriates' housekeepers and thus aided by these 'insiders' manage to sell a fair amount of fresh produce to the foreign residents of Nhyaesu on a weekly basis. Some of the children from the shantytown, not subject to school schedules would become master craftsmen. Sometimes wooden statues, metal sculptures, even model cars made from old tin cans and flip flop rubber would be offered by these 'door-to-door' sales people. Both Denzil and Xavier were proud owners of incredibly detailed model vehicles: a Mercedes Benz; a fire engine with movable ladder; a low-loader truck, each one very skillfully made. The boys pulled around these toys, usually over a foot in length, wherever they went, the vehicles holding up surprisingly well for months until they fell eventually apart and had to be replaced.

All in all, life in Ghana for Albert and his family had been idyllic by Western standards, even with the occasional food and petrol shortages: holidays spent in Elmina (a small town on the coast); in Amadzofe (a village in the mountains, just above the cloud line); trips abroad every year; truly the Lewis' had lived the good life. The overly-competitive and greedy nature of Western society, the rat race that both Albert and Jodie remembered from England had been gladly forgotten and, after seventeen years in Ghana, reluctantly re-entered into.

Chapter 11: Our children, our future

So much time had passed and so much had been left unsaid. All these months, years that had passed had left Xavier with so many bitter memories, most of which he hoped would be forgotten all too soon, or at least entombed deep out of reach in his subconscious.

A child, an innocent, unknowing, all learning creature takes over one's life and one must rapidly adjust to accommodate this new being into daily existence.

Xavier, weary from a twelve hour shift at the restaurant, holding his son carefully in his arms, gazed at the helpless being; stared deep into Oliver's bright blue eyes and began to cry. Tears formed quickly and ran down Xavier's cheeks dropping onto Oliver's exposed calf; the infant kicked out with both of his chubby pink legs and muttered some kind of protest. Katie called from the bedroom for Xavier to bring Oliver to her. "He's hungry. Come on, bring him here Xav!"

It was funny, Xavier thought, how these desolate hours, once reserved for love-making or fridge-raiding, were now allocated entirely for baby care: feeding and changing and calming and changing again! Xavier carried Oliver to his mother and after getting himself a drink from the kitchen, headed out onto the balcony. A gentle, warm breeze wafted through Xavier's recently bleached hair as he stepped out into the refreshing, eucalyptus perfume laden air of this Northern Californian summer night.

Lighting a cigarette, the first in six or seven months, Xavier closed his eyes and drew the smoke into his lungs. It had been a good stretch, he thought, longer than he had expected. Katie had quit the day the pregnancy was confirmed: the day the party ended. The smoke struck his lungs like the hot, putrid smoke from a funeral pyre would burn the lungs of a family in mourning. It was as much as he could do to stop himself from vomiting, swallowing hard, over and over, and trying to recall happy memories. Xavier tipped his glass of Guinness to his lips and drank. He recalled the first time he'd experienced this condition; twenty-one years old, living away from home for the first time, bearing the scars of adolescent depression on his forearm like a concentration camp prisoner branded with an identification number. Glancing briefly at his forearm, Xavier saw himself in the ventilation shaft that he had clambered into in a drunken stupor, pulling himself deep into the blackness after somehow replacing the grate.

Before the peaceful humming of the fans buried in the basement of St. Mary's College had worked their calming magic on Xavier, he had sliced open his left forearm, carving an 'X' over and over again with the razor-sharp blade of the pen-knife his father had given him one Christmas. He had then licked gently at the wound as a stray dog would pathetically lick an open sore.

In the months that followed, Xavier had fallen further and further into a soul-destroying depression, a descent that was accelerated by his move to Sheffield to work as a recording studio engineer, leaving behind his parents and close-knit group of friends, (friends who unknowingly, through their unconditional love and companionship, had kept Xavier above the line of dangerous self destruction).

Moving in with a friend that owned a top floor apartment near the city center – a friend who, as it turned out, became a very bad influence on him – Xavier had begun spending the majority of evenings writing somber poetry, composing dark, depressing music and drinking more and more as the weeks passed. On his days off from work at the recording studio, his room-mate would send him out shopping, usually telling him to go to Manchester or Liverpool, with a friend's credit card and a list of things he wanted: clothes, CDs, small electronics. Upon returning, laden with hundreds of pounds worth of stuff, his room-mate would call the owner of the credit card who would then call in his card as lost thus avoiding any charges that Xavier had run up that day; sometimes he would be in possession of a credit card for a few days while the owner was away on a verifiable trip. In the evenings Xavier would sit on the window ledge high above the bright lights of the city gazing out, an emptiness in his eyes as though in a deep trance. As the months passed and the voices screaming "Suicide!" grew clearer, Xavier had fled home leaving behind the horrors of loneliness and the threat of jail: during one 'shopping trip' to London, at Euston Station attempting to buy some rail passes to use on future pillages, Xavier had been busted.

"Mr. Numwar, what does the P stand for?" The clerk behind the counter, staring at him intently through the thick glass partition, had the phone pressed to his right ear, and was holding the credit card in his left hand. Xavier was sweating, his mind racing; "turn and run!" it told him, "just turn and fucking run!" There was no way in hell that the man would be able to get out of the ticket office fast enough but it was still too risky.

Xavier had met the owner of this particular credit card only briefly in a pub. As his name suggested, he was indeed Indian.

"Parmie", Xavier blurted, desperately trying to recall his name.

The clerk spoke into the phone; his cockney accent and his crisp, pressed blue shirt were annoying Xavier. "This'll only take a minute," he said, looking at a very sweaty, fidgety, Caucasian-looking Mr. Numwar.

"I'm just going to make a phone call. I'll be right back," Xavier said, as calm as a cucumber. Without waiting for the clerk to respond, Xavier turned and walked insouciantly to the block of pay phones in the center of the terminal. As soon as he was inside the hall of phones that stood in the center of the railway terminal and hidden from the clerk's view, Xavier pushed through the irritating hoards of people who were standing around like penguins in a zoo to the opening on the far side and broke into a run. He ran through the streets of London until he could run no more.

Upon his return to Durham, Albert and Jodie had immediately seen the change in Xavier and had offered him all the love and support they could, but ultimately had avoided bringing up the subject of depression during conversations with their son, conversations that Xavier would vehemently cut short in his stubbornness and state of denial if he felt pressured in any way.

The Guinness tasted good, and so with his stomach now settled, Xavier quickly emptied his glass and got himself another from the fridge; he knew that Katie would be calling him to bed as soon as Oliver had fallen back off to sleep. He knew also that he wouldn't be able to get to sleep unless he was drunk: he was worried about the reaction his

93

parents were going to have when they read the letter and poem that he had just sent off.

A few mornings later, with the phone resting on his ear, his brother's deep, calming voice on the line soothing his pounding head after he had been rudely awakened by the loud ringing, Xavier cracked open his eyes and looked over at the fuzzy, red numbers glowing on the alarm clock: '8:32'.

"Sorry to wake you bro', but I needed to talk to you." It was strange to hear that his older, wiser brother needed to talk to him.

"What's up Denzil?"

"Nina is leaving me."

Xavier reached for the glass of water on the bedside table and took a drink.

"She's taking Rebecca and going back to Birmingham. She has a job lined up and wants a divorce." Xavier could hear his brother's voice wavering. "Has she called you?"

Xavier bit his bottom lip. "No. Why is she leaving you?"

"She says she can't take any more shit from me. She reckons some woman called her and told her I was shagging her. Nina believed her and called me just now."

"Who's the woman?"

"I don't know bro'. Someone's trying to mess up my life."

Xavier thought back to when his brother had explained to him that husbands have certain rights that their wives have to accept and respect. That's the way it was in Central

94

America. Women had created the institution of marriage in an attempt to corral men into submission.

"You don't know who this woman is?" Xavier asked again, his brain still clouded by the beer from the previous night.

"I have no idea! Nina's leaving for her parents today and then flying to England next week sometime." Denzil sounded angry.

"What are you going to do?"

"I don't know bro'." There was a long silence. "I'm going to phone mum and dad now. I love you bro'. Bye."

Xavier placed the phone back in its cradle and rolled onto his back. He shrugged his shoulders as Katie leant over to kiss his cheek. "What's going on sweetie?"

"Nothing!" Xavier answered angrily. He stumbled into the bathroom and splashed his face with cool, refreshing water.

"What's wrong Xavier?" Katie called from the bedroom intuitively. Xavier was silent for a while as he composed his reply.

"I don't love you any more." He swallowed hard and looked up at his reflection in the mirror. His puffy, bloodshot eyes stared vehemently back at him disappointed with the wreck they saw before them. Katie was beside him in a second, her eyes brimming with tears. "What?" she blazed, tugging at Xavier's left arm.

"I'm sorry. I think that you're making me unhappy. It's like you're ruining my life!" Xavier gripped the edge of the sink and shut his eyes tight, causing a stream of tears to run down his cheeks. In the empty silence, he thought he could hear his blood coursing through his veins. The slap rang loudly and painfully in Xavier's head. His right cheek began throbbing immediately. "Fuck you!" yelled Katie as she fled from the brightness of the bathroom.

Xavier clenched his fists and in one movement, spun around and punched the wall behind him as hard as he could. With his heart and fist screaming, he grabbed the closest thing he could find, a bottle of Johnson's baby powder, and threw it into the bedroom. The top of the plastic container exploded off with a dull 'pop!' as the bottle hit the wall at the far side of the bed, showering the bedside table and chest of drawers with its fine white contents.

Chapter 12: Life goes on

Albert sipped his coffee and looked over at Jodie.

"We can't blame ourselves." He bit into the imported After Eight mint chocolate wafer. Jodie put down her mug of coffee and stared for a moment at the sugar bowl sitting on a plate in the middle of the dining table.

"If there's pain in our family, it's not to due to us withholding of love from our sons," she said as she reached for an After Eight. "Nothing that we did was wrong. I don't have an answer to all this."

Albert turned to look out of the window. The lights on the mountainside glowed softly like distant stars. Without saying a word, he got up from his chair and left the room.

Sitting down at his desk in the study, Albert leafed through the recent mail; he found the last letter that Xavier had sent and pulled out the poem he'd sent along with a letter containing the latest news.

'My Son'

'Sometimes, things don't seem as good as they should be.
Life takes a turn, so suddenly you're thrown off course.
Your arm screams in pain as you slice the flesh
with the knife that your father bought.

It's a very different day. It's a thought provoking,
sobriety induced time that sucks you into self-analysis.
The scars on your arm say so much about your pain
and yet you pull them away from a loved ones' kiss.

Heart sunken in confusion, away from friends, the end
seems so close to you. Could you ever make amends?
Or would that send you back to the past?
Cast your vote, there's no cost.

Lost in the fog of drunkenness, scraping violently for
freedom,
inflicting bleeding wounds in your own private
Armageddon.
Is this my life away from you, my son?
So young. And you, my wife…gone.

Loneliness consumes my being, drags me into a darkness
I despise. There's no compromise. Is the future with you
and my son? Is loving you all that I need? Spread your
wings

and make for the seas. I would follow. Could this be true?'

The words bit hard into Albert's heart. Jodie appeared in the doorway.

"What are you doing?"

"I'm going to write to Xavier and say that I'm sorry."

"Sorry for what?" Jodie put her hands on Albert's tense shoulders.

Albert folded the sheet of paper and slipped it back in the envelope along with Xavier's letter. "I feel like he needs help."

"I think you're forgetting that he's an adult now. He can make his own decisions, good or bad. If he has decided that he has to leave Katie, then we have to respect that decision. All we can do is give him our love and support." Jodie stroked her husband's soft, dark hair and then turned to walk away.

"We're going to lose our grandchildren! We'll never see Oliver and Rebecca again. You think that's okay?" Albert got up suddenly and pushed past Jodie. A moment later, she heard the back door slam shut loudly.

Sitting on the dusty, cracked stone floor of the chapel in the ruined Bellapais abbey, Albert raised his hands to his face and wiped the tears from his eyes. Pain is strange when it comes from this deep within your soul, he thought; it rips open your heart revealing hidden memories, making you stop and take stock of your life. "Why Lord? Why?"

Albert sobbed into his hands. The musty odor inside the crumbling thirteenth century chapel was oddly comforting and Albert suddenly remembered the storage room below his study at the house in Nhyaesu: Xavier, Denzil and their friends would scamper around in this unused, doorless room singing and shouting at the tops of their voices, playing games like 'Ring-a-ring-a-roses', or simply enjoying the fabulous acoustics of the room. Albert would sit back in his chair in the study above and listen to the muted echoing of the young, developing voices that reverberated through the walls. "We did nothing wrong," he said to himself as he straightened up and dried his eyes with his handkerchief. The faded painting of St. Hilarion sporting a golden halo and carrying a crystal encrusted scepter, holding up against the salty coastal winds surprisingly well, smiled down from the wall opposite. Albert breathed in deeply, the air thick with memories, and carefully stood up.

Jodie was washing the dishes from dinner when Albert reached the house they were renting a little way outside of Girne (formally known as Kyrenia), a large town on the coast in Northern Cyprus. He heard her humming a tune he recognized as one of Xavier's compositions. Quietly walking into the kitchen, Albert stood and watched Jodie for a minute before sneaking up behind her. She gasped as he put his arms around her waist. He leant forward and kissed the back of her head. Through the window above

100

the sink, he could see Daisy on the perimeter wall looking in at the two of them. Jodie put down the saucepan she'd been scrubbing, wiped her hands briefly on the tea towel lying on the counter and turned around. She embraced Albert, squeezing him tightly. A smile crossed his face as he felt a beautiful warmth settle over him.

Albert and Jodie had been on the island for almost a year: Albert had been offered the post of Director of the Architecture Department at the International University of Lefke which had recently gone through a quite substantial enlargement (the Turkish Government believing that by investing money in the University – thereby attracting more professors and students from overseas – the United Nations would look more favorably on the resident Turks; the ultimate goal was to have the northern side incorporated into the UN) Life was comfortable for Albert and Jodie; Jodie had built up a small but growing group of piano students, Albert was well respected in his position; and putting the ethnic tensions aside, (the Greek Cypriots would gladly have the Turks thanklessly booted off the island) the Lewis' enriched their lives with the fabulous Mediterranean cuisines, the wonderful Cypriot music and weekend trips to destinations steeped in the great history that Cyprus has: the monasteries of St. Barnabas and St. Hilarion; the ancient towns of Famagusta and Nikosia; the ruins of numerous settlements (from the middle-ages) along the Karpas peninsular.

Xavier, ignoring the talcum powder that lay like volcanic ash over the furniture by the wall, fell onto the canopy bed. As he landed on the mattress, the rush of air blew some of the powder up off the bedside table and Xavier watched, hypnotized, as the fine white powder swirled around and floated gently back down. He could hear Katie in the living room talking to Oliver; her voice was trembling.

"This jacket will keep you warm Boody. We'll have breakfast at Molly's. You like it there. They have that big fish tank, remember?"

Oliver was babbling in his usual fashion. Xavier pulled the pillow around his ears as more tears welled up in his eyes. After hearing the front door closing, he rolled into the center of the queen size bed and began crying softly into the pillow.

Xavier was still lying on the bed when Katie and Oliver returned. He watched as Katie gently laid the sleeping baby on the bed, placing a pillow on either side of him to keep him from rolling off the bed or into Xavier's space. She leant over and kissed the tip of her husband's nose.

"I love you Sweetie" she whispered. Xavier, on occasion, could forget just how beautiful Katie was: a petite young lady with wavy dark-blonde hair, almost turquoise blue-green eyes, a perfect figure that looked so alluring in a bikini and a polite and considerate nature that had been commented on by many people. Her devotion to Xavier was impenetrable and unlike anything he'd encountered before in his relationships. He followed Katie with his eyes as she walked around the bed. She carefully lay down on the bed and embraced him. Oliver rolled over, his perfectly formed head coming to rest against Xavier's left hand. Xavier stroked his son's fine golden ringlets with his index finger. He turned to look at Katie; tears rolled down his cheeks and they kissed. Lovemaking as a substitute for discussion had always been an easy way out of an emotionally charged situation for Xavier and so with his son sleeping soundly next to him, Xavier mutely fell in love with his wife once again.

"I'll put in for a transfer to Miami. You can look after Oliver until you find a job and then I'll bid my schedule around yours." Katie was lying on the bed nursing Oliver as Xavier came out of the bathroom. He finished drying himself off and began dressing for work. "I know we'll be happier back in Florida. It's too expensive for us here," she continued. Oliver pulled off her nipple and looked at his father.

"Hey Boody! Pappy's going to work now. Are you going to be good for mammy?" Oliver mumbled something and then went back to his lunch. Xavier checked his tie in the bathroom mirror. "We'll talk about it tomorrow. Maybe that's the best thing to do but..." He turned off the bathroom light, "I'll never match this salary there. And what'll we do with all our stuff? We're not going to sell it all and start over again. We've done that once already!"

As he sat in the luxurious cabin of the perfectly maintained cabin of the nineteen sixty-nine Cadillac Coupe Deville that he had persuaded Katie to invest some money in, waiting for it's enormous (four hundred and seventy cubic inches!) engine to warm up, Xavier felt a smile forming. Pressing the accelerator for a second, he checked for the puff of smoke in the rear-view mirror. "Power!" he said to himself as he slowly reversed the seventeen feet long American engineering masterpiece out of the parking space. He loved this car: he loved cleaning and polishing it: he loved gazing at its long, sleek, golden lines; it's shining chrome bumpers: he loved driving this car, feeling its limitless power and watching all the heads turn as he cruised by. This car – the same age as Katie – had been the most reliable of any of the automobiles the Lewis family had ever owned, including the Peugeots that Albert had always been a fan of. Katie, who disliked the Cadillac because of its ridiculous length and obscene petrol consumption, had bought herself a Jeep Wrangler soon after her pregnancy had been confirmed, citing the need for a 'small run-around' car for herself. As Xavier pulled into the parking lot in front of the Sahara restaurant, he noticed that his smile had disappeared. Acknowledging the (mostly Mexican) cooks as he walked past the open-style kitchen, he felt the tears welling up again. He clumsily unlocked the door to the tiny manager's office and quickly slipped inside. Locking the door, he sat down and covered his face with his hands.

"Won't she be worried if you don't call?" John asked as he walked over to the bar with their empty glasses.

"I don't want to wake Oliver up. I'll call in the morning. She'll understand. Anyway, I don't have to..." the phone interrupted Xavier. "If that's her, tell her I'm showing the cleaners around and I'll be home in a little bit."

A divorcee and a father, John could see the void in Xavier's heart. He reluctantly lied to his colleague's wife and hung up the phone at the bar.

"She won't be happy Xav. I think you should go home soon."

"Just pour the bloody beer John!" Xavier hated people offering their opinions to him about his marriage. Nobody knew how it really was: he had it pretty tough; Katie was too demanding and was starting to wear his patience thin. Frequent affirmations like these exacerbated the problem; John recognized this stage clearly.

"I'm leaving after this beer Xav," he announced as he returned from the bar with two pints of Bass.

"I'll have one more just to kill a little more time; Katie will be asleep by then." Xavier was a true Aires and as stubborn as they came.

Opening the front door, Xavier saw Katie kneeling on the carpet and Oliver a few feet in front of her, his head erect, desperately trying to crawl to his mother. "Shit!" Xavier said under his breath. Oliver, hearing the door open, immediately turned his head and smiled up at him. Avoiding the inevitable confrontation, Xavier hastily disappeared into the bedroom.

"Do you think you're clever?" Katie asked with unmistakable malice: she was standing in the doorway. "What did you hope to achieve? I was about to call the Police!" She stopped speaking for a moment; her eyes like some wild animal's. "You need help!" The door slammed behind her as she went back into the living room.

After talking to the Doctor, Xavier felt like a valve had been opened slightly, easing the pressure inside his heart. He folded the prescription in half, put it in his back pocket and left the Doctor's office. The elevator door closed and Xavier began crying again. The drive to the pharmacy seemed to last an eternity: this must be a dream, he thought; the cars passing by appeared to be floating just above the road like hovercraft; the deep growling of the Cadillac's engine sounded like monks singing Gregorian chant. "I can't believe it's come to this!" Xavier kept saying to himself as he waited for the Pharmacist to give him his Prozac. An appointment had been made for him to begin seeing a therapist for counseling that would eventually, combined with the Prozac fix his 'problem'.

That was the plan. However, no one had prepared Xavier for the horrors of self-analysis and self-reflection and so Xavier soon shut off his subconscious mind from the probing questions of the therapist and completed his sessions relatively painlessly and walked away with a new classification. He wasn't depressed; he was suffering from 'adjustment disorder'. To his friends and work-mates, once he had persuaded himself that this was an enviable thing, he proudly spoke of his new affliction, as a child would show off a medal or trophy.

But now, sitting on the bed with the first two pills in his hand, Xavier looked down at the mind-altering drug and, reading the print on the capsules, breathed in deeply. "Save me!" he prayed before he swallowed.

Chapter 13: Zimbabwe

Xavier lit another cigarette and leant back in the yellow vinyl café chair; the ashtray was already overflowing. 'I must slow down with the fags,' he said to himself before remembering that he'd bought two packs on the way home from work. The balcony he was sitting on looked out onto a tropical garden planted with tall, slender palms. A pair of pigeons had recently built a nest near the top of the one closest to the balcony in the cluster of its branches. The globe lamps on thin, eight feet tall poles illuminated the pathways around the trees. An unusually cool December breeze suddenly blew through the mosquito netting sending a shiver down Xavier's spine. Katie was back in Durham (at her mother's house in the village of Brandon, three miles south of the city center) to be with her mother: Elizabeth had been diagnosed with acute myeloid leukemia and was undergoing chemotherapy at Dryburn Hospital. The day before Thanksgiving, Katie had called Xavier at work and pleaded with him to come home immediately. Driving his wife and son to Miami airport two hours later, Xavier had begun thinking that this break would help his marriage. He and Katie had been slowly growing apart since the move from Burlingame. The anti-depressants seemed to have stopped working and Xavier had felt his emotional state worsening. Standing very still beside the Jeep, hands in his pockets, ignoring the impatient horn of the car that was waiting for the space he'd parked in, Xavier had watched as Katie and Oliver disappeared into the crowded United Airlines' check-in hall. Katie's farewell tears had touched him briefly, but as he drove away, fighting through the crazy pre-Thanksgiving Day airport traffic, Xavier had blocked out his weakening emotions and urgently headed home.

The sealed white envelope containing the latest letter to his parents lay on the upturned cardboard box that Xavier used as a side table (for his beer and the ashtray) on the balcony. Opening another bottle of Grolsch, enjoying the fresh 'phshh!' sound it produced as the hinged ceramic top popped off, Xavier looked down at the pathways below illuminated by the orange-yellow globe lamps; they appeared to be undulating ever so slightly like cold snakes. Tipping the bottle of Grolsch to his lips, toying with his Swiss Army knife in his left hand, Xavier thought back to his night in the ventilation shaft at St. Mary's College. He put his beer down and opened up the two-inch blade: the steel flashed enticingly in front of him, reflecting the light from the living room behind him as it moved to the scar on his left arm. Xavier pressed it down hard onto his forearm enjoying the anticipation.

Xavier, Katie and Oliver had moved from Burlingame to Fort Lauderdale the previous July; Elizabeth paying for all their furniture, belongings and the Jeep to be shipped across country. Xavier had soon found a job as Front Desk supervisor at a hotel on the beach, a job he was enjoying – finally! Life was still hard for him to cope with, but the pills made it tolerable. Since Katie and Oliver had left, Xavier had spent his evenings and days off drinking, acerbating his depression. Nights like these had become more frequent over the last couple of weeks especially.

Words began forming in his head into an expression of his pathetic emotional state; a description of which he'd tried to convey earlier in the letter to his parents but had eventually skirted. Xavier paused to listen as his beer-soaked brain attempted to formulate the mish-mash of words into something coherent, the steel blade waiting eagerly to do its work. Looking up, Xavier saw the three lights – red, white and green – of a small airplane moving across the dark sky, hidden for a few seconds as they went behind the branches of the pigeon's palm tree and then continuing on their silent journey until they disappeared behind the roof-top of the adjacent apartment building. Lifting the steel away from his arm, Xavier inhaled sharply and closed up the penknife. He picked up the note pad and pen that were on the floor to his right and began spewing his anger and pain instead onto the yellow ruled paper.

'It's a lie!'

'It's a lie! It's a lie!
It's a sigh
from deep within my soul.
It's a lie! It's a lie!

It's a wave goodbye
from the departure gate
as you fly away with my baby.
Tears that are forming

are for him, not you my lady!
The look; the love you see in my eyes
is for my child.
It's a lie! It's a lie!

It's a cry
from my heartstrings.
It's a lie! It's a lie!
It's a shrug of my shoulders

as I shy away
from your affections.
Fears that are growing are for the future
away from my child.'

The computer finally, after a typically long pause, acknowledged that the email had been sent. Albert logged out and turned to Jodie, standing on his right in the University library. "I'm sure he's okay, darling! He's strong enough to get through this. We'll call Katie tonight to see how things are with Elizabeth and see if Xavier has called her." One of his students appeared and after first greeting Jodie, shyly approached Albert.

"Excuse me Professor Lewis, I'm sorry to interrupt you, but I would like to invite you and Mrs. Lewis to lunch this Sunday, if you are free."

Albert pushed the chair back away from the desk, rose and shook Joseph's outstretched hand. "Thank you Joseph, I don't think we have any plans: do we dear?"

"No. That would be lovely. Thank you Joseph" Jodie responded. "How's the baby?"

"Very well Mrs. Lewis. She's growing up too fast. You won't recognize her. Well, I have some research to do for the last paper you gave us Professor Lewis. I must go. You can come to my house any time after eleven o'clock. Goodbye Mrs. Lewis; Professor Lewis." Joseph bowed slightly before turning to leave.

Joseph Mlalazi was one of Albert's more promising students at the new National University of Arts and Technology in Bulawayo. A quiet, gentle man in his early thirties – almost the same age as Xavier, but so much more focused and mature Albert thought – Joseph had scored

112

almost perfect marks in all of the exams the previous semester and his presentation of rural housing options at the highly acclaimed Student's Day (that Albert taken upon himself to organize) had received much praise from the invited guests – a large selection of local architects, University staff and board members. Jodie and Joseph's young wife Shari, a statuesque Ndebele girl with a large afro that she usually kept in tight braids, had very quickly become close friends; Shari affectionately called Jodie 'Auntie' even when they were out in public together. Jodie had learnt to prepare some delicious local dishes during the last few months; recipes that she practiced on Albert much to his delectation; his favorite to date was a soup made with vegetables cooked in oil strained from palm nuts, very similar to palm nut stew, a traditional Ghanaian dish.

Escaping the increasing political unrest in Cyprus when his contract at the International University of Lefke ended, Albert had happily accepted the post of Head of Department at the School of Architecture at the National University of Science and Technology in Bulawayo (the second capital of Zimbabwe) and following a brief holiday in England, he and Jodie had moved there; back to Africa! This was a great opportunity he thought; the fairly new University was still growing, both in size and in prestige and beginning to attract students from neighboring countries. Now settled, three months later, into a very comfortable house – a beautiful, large, colonial style bungalow with an expansive, walled garden planted with lush, tropical flora and fauna in the suburbs of Bulawayo – Albert and Jodie finally felt at peace. Although for the most part a Mediterranean paradise, Cyprus had always had the discouraging shadow of political and ethnic unrest hanging over it, and even though she kept her fears hidden from everyone, Jodie at times felt uneasy when walking or driving alone. Little was she to know that in a short while, she would be feeling even more timorous in Zimbabwe.

Albert, his eye attached to the viewfinder of the camera – an aging Olympus SLR that he'd bought many years ago from Robertson's Photography in Durham – focused carefully as the elephants sauntered past not more than ten feet away. The guide, a handsome young Zimbabwean man, was speaking very softly, so softly that Jodie could not hear him over her tinnitus. Hwange National Park was one of Zimbabwe's best and most visited – the country has numerous Wild Game Parks – and had become a frequent weekend destination for them. "What did he say?" Jodie whispered as she pulled a dainty, white handkerchief embroidered with tiny daisies from a pocket on her long, blue denim skirt and patted the perspiration that was collecting in her graceful eyebrows.
"I wasn't listening darling. Sorry. I'm trying to get a photograph of the matriarch." Albert was engrossed in his camera's viewfinder. Jodie turned to look towards the couple from South Africa standing on the other side of the

guide who, with his arm on the woman's shoulder was now animatedly pointing at the area of bush that the herd of elephants had come from. The lone painted hunting dog that the guide had pointed out earlier was crouched low in the yellow grass; it's over-sized round ears cocked. The young woman – a very pretty, tall and slender model type with shiny, auburn, shoulder blade length hair – was saying something to her husband, obviously quite rich due to his marked unattractiveness and weight, and appeared to be pulling him back; the man, the back of his light blue short-sleeved shirt stuck to his sweaty back, seemed to be leaning forward as though about to start running. Jodie could hear the guide speaking with a thick local accent that she could normally understand, but still could not make out a word that he was saying. The young South African man suddenly turned to his wife, raised his right arm high in the air and brought it down with a great slap across her left cheek.

"Albert! Look! He just hit her!" Jodie tugged at Albert's arm.

"Jodie!" Albert, almost pouting, turned to see what was so urgent. "I almost had it! She was looking at us and the baby was in the picture too. What's going on?" His forehead was deeply furrowed.

Just then, from a little way behind the group of seven that Albert and Jodie were a part of, the roar of a diesel engine erupted. The opened-topped stretched Land Rover, painted with large zebra stripes, lurched forward, its tires throwing up clouds of orange dust into the sweltering midday air. The man in the passenger seat, a middle-aged white man with shoulder length, wavy, blonde hair was aiming a black rifle out of the window in the direction of the group of visitors and shouting to the driver in Afrikaans.

"What's going on Albert?" Jodie was panicking.

"It's okay dear! They won't harm us," Albert said reassuringly with his head held high and shoulders pulled back like a kangaroo defending its territory. He was dressed in his favorite safari suit, with matching hat. (Xavier had always thought his father, when dressed up like this, looked as though he'd stepped out of Conrad's *Heart of Darkness.)* Just as he was about to begin puffing up his chest, the Land Rover, bouncing across the rough terrain like a child's Tonka truck in a sand pit, veered off to the left of the group, the white man with the rifle, his blonde hair blowing about wildly, desperately trying to keep the gun steady.

What happened in the next few seconds was like a scene from a film played in slow motion before Jodie's eyes: a deafening shot rang out as the rifle went off; there were two or three screams in unison; everyone ducked; the guide fell to the ground pulling the woman who'd been slapped with him; Albert grasped Jodie's waist and pulled her in to his arms; shouting something in Afrikaans, the man who'd slapped his wife fell on top of the her and the guide; the Land Rover, without slowing at all, crashed into the bush

116

in the vicinity of the guide's interest; the painted hunting dog let out a high-pitched howl as it sprinted off; a large lion with sandy-yellow fur sprang out from the bush to the left of the bouncing (and now braking) zebra-striped Land Rover and darted off into another area of bush about fifteen yards away from Albert and Jodie.

"Everyone alright?" the white marksman from the Land Rover, dressed very similarly to Albert (minus the hat) and proudly holding his shiny black rifle across his chest, asked once everyone had calmed down and stopped talking. The woman who'd been slapped, her previously pale cheek now quite red and sore looking raised her arm. "Go ahead young lady" he responded, motioning to her with the rifle. He spat as she began to speak, the ball of saliva hitting the dirt with a soft thud and raising a small puff of dust from the scorched earth.

"I'd like to leave now please." She couldn't have been more than twenty years old Jodie thought as she watched the proceedings from a few feet away, comfortable in the shade of the baobab tree that she, Albert and the guide were standing under. The other two tourists, Ruby and Derek Patterson from Nottingham, with whom Albert and Jodie had chatted on the drive out, were climbing into the back of the Land Rover that had parked alongside them all. They had come to Zimbabwe to celebrate their silver wedding anniversary: they'd lived in the country for many years when it had been Rhodesia but had returned to

117

England when power had been handed over to the Africans. The husband of the young woman, standing behind her, was glaring at the guide as he drank from a bottle of water he'd been carrying in a sling over his shoulder. He shot Albert and Jodie a disdainful look before turning to speak to his fellow countryman who was wiping the barrel of his rifle with a bandana that had been tucked into his back pocket.

"They're ruining the whole country! It's the same back home; they think they can run these great countries, but it was our people who built everything, designed the towns. These people..." he flicked his head in their direction, "are destroying everything we built!"

The blonde man nodded in agreement and spat again. "Mugabe's a bloody bastard! The fucking veterans took my farm! I wanted to shoot the whole fucking lot of them! I came to this country when I was twenty-six, built a farm, worked on it every bloody day for twenty years, and Mugabe tells them to take it from me! I'll kill the bloody bastards! "

Jodie's tinnitus couldn't shield her ears from the conversation the two white men were having. She hated these bigots and their angry words that she encountered every day. It was true that the President was doing a dreadful job at running the country: the economy was in shambles; crime was out of the control of the police, a corrupt bunch of lazy men who most of the time turned a blind eye to crimes against the white populous – Albert and Jodie had already had their home burglarized whilst away on weekend trips to Kyle View in the Eastern Highlands twice in the year they'd been in Zimbabwe, the night watchmen, replaced after each break-in, asleep while the thieves were at work. But the attitude that the majority of white Zimbabweans were developing was not going to help matters in any way, Jodie believed, on the contrary, it was making life more difficult than it should be, especially for those (mostly foreigners) with more liberal views.

"I'll fucking kill him!" The young South African scowled at the guide, who, with his head bowed, was staring at the dry, yellow, cracked earth around his bare feet, which Jodie noticed were as dry, yellow, cracked and dusty as the ground they stood on.

Two comforting cups of tea and a piece of home-made Key lime pie (from a recipe Jodie had found on a postcard in the tiny gift shop in Key West airport) later, Albert folded the newspaper in half on his lap and took a deep breath of warm late afternoon air filled with a myriad of floral scents. "Let's call Katie and see how everything's going."

Chapter 14: Cold Turkey

"I think he's just lonely. And he's stopped taking the Prozac." Katie's voice was even quieter than it normally was. Listening intently on the second phone in Albert's study, Jodie began worrying immediately.

"Do you think he should be coming off the drug so quickly Katie?"

"He doesn't have enough money to get the prescription filled. He told me he'd get some St. John's Wort; that should help a bit. We talked about him coming back here. It would be much easier for all of us if he did. Oliver misses him so much." Her voice was beginning to falter. "He said that he just needs to sell the Jeep and the furniture and then he'll come over."

Jodie looked up at the framed photograph of Oliver that Xavier had sent in his last letter; she smiled back at her grandson, beaming, his beautiful blue eyes bright with excitement, leaning over a low, dark wooden coffee table.

"It must be so hard for him to be away from Oliver and you especially as this will be Oliver's first Christmas. Do you think he'll really come back to Durham?" Jodie flinched as the words came out. Without waiting for

Katie's reply, she digressed. "Xavier will do what he knows is best for all of you. How's your mother Katie? Poor thing. Please give her our love. We hope…"

Listening to his wife's vain attempts to cover her faux pas, Albert interjected from the phone in the living room; "You said that your mum would be out of hospital for Christmas. No doubt you're all looking forward to that!"

"Yes Albert, we are. At least she'll have one day that she can feel normal. She's going to get a wig." Katie was trying to focus on the swerve in the conversation.

"Well, please do give your mum our love and love to you and Oliver: we're thinking of you all. We'll call you again soon." Albert breathed a sigh of relief as he walked into the study. "We have to be very careful darling. Xavier's getting worse!"

"He's not growing up, is he? I wonder what's wrong with him. He said in that email that he'd started biting his nails again. Why would he tell us that?" Jodie looked across at Daisy, possibly the world's most widely traveled cat, immutably licking her fur as she lay on the wicker chair in the corner of the large study; the walls lined with bookcases filled with books of various sizes; books that had followed the Lewis' around the world for the last twenty years; books covering such diverse subjects as the search for Atlantis, Middle-Eastern cooking, Sufism and European Railways. There was also a book of love poems in Spanish by Denzil Lewis awaiting translation.

The steel felt icy cold. Carefully sliding the blade along his skin, Xavier ground his back teeth as the tender scar was gently sliced open. 'Do you know anything about cutters? Look it up sometime mate,' Xavier had written recently in an email to a friend in Grand Cayman as cry for help. A week later, with no response to his appeal, he had phoned his closest friend in Durham, Charlie Hernandez, to ask if he remembered the night at St. Mary's college. "I feel like I did then Charlie. I don't know what to do."

"What will you do if you come back here Xav? There's nothing here. No jobs. Nothing has changed. Nothing ever will change here! You left because of that. Remember how glad you were to get away from this shithole? It's still the same old crap! You're much better off there man. Wait till Katie and Oliver come back and everything'll be alright I bet you." Xavier's feelings of utter isolation were mollified slightly by the sound of Charlie's voice on the phone-line; these days he very rarely called anyone back home, preferring the vizard that the Internet provided. His friend's bluntness and honesty were intensely comforting and Xavier thought back to 'the good old days' in Durham when Charlie would always do his best to keep him from losing site of reality. The phone call lifted Xavier's spirits for a couple of days; days when the sky was blue again.

Wiping the blade clean with his fingers, Xavier urgently exhaled the breath he'd held for too long. Replacing the razor sharp steel in the bleeding incision, he gently cut again. His tense forearm muscle pushed hard against its assailant: Xavier shut his eyes tightly sending blood charging through his eyelids making them throb. Images began flashing in his mind: the beach at Bahia Honda in the Florida Keys; Elmina; the fields and the trees that looked like broccoli, the lakes and wet-lands passing below the small twin-engine airplane he'd flown from Fort Lauderdale to Kissimmee – precious memories from a happier past. Swiftly delving deeper, Xavier pulled up more details from his subconscious...

The twin engines of the Piper Cheyenne strained as Xavier frantically tried to pull the aircraft out of the steep dive. "Take over Edgar!" he pleaded to his roommate. His heart was racing so fast he believed he'd be dead from a heart attack before hitting the earth. The altimeter showed that they had dropped almost two thousand feet and were still losing altitude. Emerging all of a sudden from the dense cloud, seeing the horizon at the top of the right windshield, Edgar pulled hard on his stick. The engines screamed! Xavier, sweating and shaking, gladly let go of his control stick; his fingers would not straighten for a minute or so. He watched as Edgar brought the horizon level with the bottom of the windshields. "You land it!" Xavier blurted, wiping the sweat from his brow with his still stiff left hand. The one and a half hour flight from Fort Lauderdale had been wonderful; flying an airplane was more fun than Xavier had ever imagined, up until the point when he had flown the small aircraft into the dense, moisture-filled cumulonimbus cloud somewhere over Lake Okeechobee. With the attitude meter – crucial to zero-visibility flying – out of order, Xavier had quickly become disorientated, his pilot room-mate nonchalantly smoking a cigarette, and unable to detect the gradual change in positioning he had continued to steer the aircraft in a downward curve to the left.

"You did okay, considering it was your first time. Those storm clouds can be tricky." Edgar, a young English pilot who worked with Katie for Richard Branson's airline patted Xavier on the back as the two of them walked across the field to the apartment.

The pain of an open wound began to register in Xavier's mind; he opened his eyes and blinked to clear his vision. He looked at his handiwork. Blood had collected around the blade, still pressed into his forearm; the haphazard 'X' that had been there before was now obliterated by an even more haphazard 'X'; the multiple incisions were oozing blood that appeared to be almost black – three thin lines of crimson traced towards his wrist. Throwing his head backwards, Xavier lifted the blade away from his skin and lowered his arm, resting his forearm on his lap. He grinned slightly, almost imperceptibly, his jaws still taught as he watched a droplet of blood fall from the pain remover.

"The fact that there are questions is proof enough. I'm sorry Katie. I'll never lie to you again." The alcohol spoke for him. There was a long, painful silence.

"I knew this time apart wouldn't help. Do you still love me at all?" Katie was whispering; her delicate voice almost lost in the faint static on the phone line.

"I need more time to think this through Katie. I'm going to go back to California," Xavier responded purposefully. His ear lobe ached from the pressure of the phone pressed hard against it. There was another torturous drawn-out silence.

"I love you Xav. God bless." The sadness in his wife's voice sliced into him; his whole being aflame with ire. He staggered into the bathroom. As the light came on Xavier looked at the mirror. He recognized the wretched face of his long-time friend staring back with ugly, red, puffy eyes.

"Fuck you!" He spat at the mirror. "Don't hate me God!" he prayed as he urinated. He felt some of the hot liquid splatter onto his right calf and run down to his foot. Gagging suddenly as the vomit reached his throat, Xavier fell to his knees and threw up into the unclean toilet, piss still trickling from his limp penis.

Chapter 15: God sending his Angels

The inventory list was impressive. Xavier lent back in the chair and waited for the printer finish. 'Three thousand dollars to move all this shit here! At least we'll get that back,' he said to himself. (He had already forgotten that it had been his mother-in-law who had paid for the move to Fort Lauderdale.) He picked up the original list he'd made. The accomplishments of three and a half years hard work in Burlingame were mapped out on two sides of A4 paper: the queen-size canopy bed with a pillow-top orthopedic mattress (bought to ease the discomfort of pregnancy and still being paid for monthly); the six foot solid oak dining table with six chairs (snapped up at a Goodwill store for $65!); the mahogany coffee table; two sofa-sleepers; the Krups Espresso machine; Admiral bread maker; Osterizer blender; TV; stereo; CD burner; VCR; stuff; stuff; more stuff! California had been about collecting as much shit as one could possibly fit into one's home! Xavier could trace his evolution from lazy Florida beach bum into a 'keeping-up-with-the-Jones' Californian father and husband on this crumpled dog-eared sheet of paper. After distributing neat, printed copies entitled 'Moving Sale' of his once precious, now superfluous belongings amongst his work mates at the hotel, Xavier clocked out and drove home, stopping as usual for a twelve pack of Heineken and a pack of Marlboro Lights at the Circle K near the apartment complex.

The sweet perfume of the jacaranda trees, recently decorated with multi-colored lights that had been hung everywhere, filled the air as Albert and Jodie headed home. The first class recital by the Hayden Trio from Vienna at the Academy of Music in Bulawayo (sponsored by the Austrian Embassy to mark the introduction of a direct Vienna-Harare route by Austrian Airlines) had been absolutely splendid: perfectly performed pieces by Schubert, Kreisler, Hayden and Strauss had been wildly applauded by the audience. Albert steered the VW Passat into the driveway and parking close to the brick paved stoep with its arched pergola hung with grape vines, he turned to Jodie, and reaching for her right hand, smiled and looked into her smoky, light blue eyes.

"Thank you for loving me darling," he whispered.

Jodie frowned. "Why do you say that?"

"I want to make sure you always know how much I appreciate you. We've been through some very hard times and yet you've always believed in me."

"And always will dear!" Jodie opened her door and stepped out of the car leaving the window down as

127

everything thieves would want had already been taken. Albert followed his wife into their home. Helping Jodie with her coat, he leant forward and kissed her shoulder delicately.

"Let's open the Viansa Merlot."

With the London Sinfonietta's recording of Górecki's *Symphony No.3* playing quietly (just loud enough for Jodie to hear over her tinnitus) in the living room, Albert and Jodie relaxed on the large verandah in their Arne Jacobson designed wicker chairs that they had bought in Ghana in the late sixties enjoying the warm, peaceful Zimbabwean night air and Northern Californian red wine. Although Christmas was only a week away, Albert found it difficult to feel the joys of the season with his children alone for the first Christmas in their lives and so far away. Watching the flying night insects dancing excitedly about the wall lamp behind Jodie, Albert imagined a light snow flurry falling all around. He recalled the years following their move from Ghana; Christmas' the family had spent together; the boys growing up too quickly, but still excitable during the festive build up, ardent with anticipation for Christmas morning.

During the early eighties the family had spent four consecutive Christmas Holidays in London, sojourning with the retired Sisters of the Order of the Holy Trinity in their expansive, five-story house in Bloomsbury. The

O.H.T. Sisters ran the baby's home and its adjoining guesthouse in Mampong that Albert had designed, and extended their gratitude by offering the Lewis family accommodations whenever they were in London. Xavier's baptism in Kumasi had been performed by one of the Sisters and so he was always doted over during the Lewis' visits. Most of the Sisters living in the house in London had at one time or another lived in Ghana and had avidly watched Xavier grow from an infant into a young man and would continue to embarrass him with anecdotes of his childhood antics that they had witnessed during the Lewis' frequent visits to Mampong. The holidays in London added much to the great excitement of Christmas for Denzil and Xavier: the sights and sounds and smells; and the mystifying constant hubbub of the capital had a prodigious effect on the young boys after the stately repose of life in both Durham and Kumasi. London had an illimitable abundance of fascinating places to visit and explore: the Natural History Museum with its magnificent life-size dinosaur skeletons; the Science Museum and its replicas of N.A.S.A's Apollo spacecraft; Madame Tussauds wax museum (where Xavier saw his first pair of white breasts, although made from wax, none-the-less stimulating to the pubescent boy); Buckingham Palace and the puzzling inert Palace Guards; Windsor Castle (at the tea shop set up in the royal greenhouse one could get very fine freshly baked scones served with clotted cream and a variety of preserves). However, for Xavier, by far the most rousing excursion was one that Denzil (at the time eighteen years old) took him on: the two adolescent boys managed to 'escape' one chilly, overcast afternoon and after spending a couple of edifying hours experiencing the thrills that the streets and alleyways of Soho (London's famous den of iniquity) had to offer, they returned to the O.H.T. house wide-eyed and penniless. For the fourteen year old Xavier, this experience easily outshone the rapture of Christmas day that year; the year that Mr. Yellowman performed at Wembley; the year that the Lewis' spent the two weeks following Christmas Day escaping the sleet and cold in Banjul (in The Gambia).

Albert poured the last of the wine into the two glasses and carefully placed the bottle back onto the small wooden table between the chairs. He so enjoyed these warm nights (December this far south of the equator was almost mid-summer) sitting on the verandah, the aroma of French tobacco and jacaranda perfume floating in the balmy air. As Albert opened his mouth to speak he noticed that Jodie had dozed off, her chin almost touching her exposed collarbone. He put his wineglass to his nose and sniffed. His mind meandered back to Christmases past as he took a slow, smooth draught.

Christmas day in Durham – until the boys were old enough to be distracted by alternate pleasures – began with Midnight Mass in Durham Cathedral followed by a celebratory toast at home complete with home-made mince pies and then bed for a few hours before stockings hung over the fireplace were ravaged; it was not until after the lavish lunch had been cleared away did the ceremonial gift presenting begin. Denzil and Xavier had been raised to appreciate the simple pleasures of life: good food; good music; fine art; walks in the countryside; the rising or setting sun; the sound of waves breaking on the shore; the fact that money did not bring one happiness – 'It is harder for a rich man to enter the gates of Heaven than for a camel to pass through the eye of a needle' had been reiterated again and again throughout their lives, more so since moving to England – and so in compliance with these teachings, modesty was the order of the day when it came to gifts – due now, for the most part, to the fact that Albert had successively been falling deeper and deeper into a dire financial situation. Although never jealous, back at school after the holidays, Xavier found that in order to avoid being teased – as a white boy from Africa he was already somewhat of an object of ridicule – he had to embellish his Christmas present list upon hearing of his classmates' treasures: Atari video games; Scalectrix racing car sets; Commodore 64 computers; radio-controlled cars; air rifles; bicycles with hundreds of gears! During a rare period of opulence one Christmas though, Xavier asked for and received a JVC keyboard to use along with the second-hand synthesizer he had chosen for his birthday earlier that year. Thankfully for Albert and Jodie (and their neighbors), Denzil and Xavier had their bedrooms (and their own living room and bathroom) in a two story building separate to the main house as the eldest son bought himself a drum kit a couple of months later and the two pop stars would practice together almost every day!

By the very indefatigable nature of adolescence, family takes second place as children emerge from ignorant bliss into the enticing world of self-discovery and self-dependency. Parents can merely stand in the wings as their hurriedly developing offspring, losing the satori of youth, discover the infinite pleasures available to them in the arcane melodrama of young-adulthood, and so Albert and Jodie could do nothing but watch as first Denzil and then Xavier slipped out from under their hearth-rug of careful, loving parenting. Christmas together as a family was the final bridge across the ambiguous extremities of the Lewis family unit that the young men traversed, heading into the thick, abstruse jungle that lay between them and responsibility. From this deleterious and facetious quagmire, Denzil eventually emerged some years later, an estimable, strong and wise man. Xavier however, insofar as Albert could see, was still trapped inside, unable to escape its claws.

Xavier pressed the phone harder against his ear. Lying on his side, the tears streamed unhampered onto the pillow. "Right now your mother needs you more than I do. I still need some time alone." The sound of Oliver's intermittent babbling in the background sliced deep wounds into Xavier's heart. In the years to come he would look back at this time in his life, these mistakes he made, with an esoteric wild anger, and a debilitating self-hatred that consumed his soul.

"But this is his first Christmas. And I see how much he misses his pappy every day." Katie hoped this would kindle some feelings in her husband.

"Don't come back Katie! I've got to go. Give Oliver a kiss for me." He refused to allow himself to been drawn into her web. A sudden, strong gust of wind blew through the open window causing the off-white vertical blinds to swing violently, clacking noisily against themselves and the bed frame. Xavier turned his eyes towards the sound and looked out at the deep blue sky. The blinds, just as quickly as they began swinging, were still. He heard a burst of excited bird song. A penetrating coldness began enveloping his body, filling him with a feeling of dread: it was not the time to die! Rolling onto his back, he saw a thick, heavy board descending over his tomb, plunging him into a sudden, horrifying blackness as it was maneuvered into place; felt the sides of the sarcophagus tremor as an iron nail was hammered into the imprisoning lid, sealing it shut.

"I love you Xavier," Katie's voice whispered from the receiver. Another nail was hammered into place.

"Xavier?"

Silence.

"Xavier?" His wife's voice grew fainter. Her soft, sweet calling dissipated into the emptiness. Xavier's whole body began trembling uncontrollably; the blackness like a thick, putrid mud enfolded him, swallowing his wretched, shaking corpse, restraining him from any kind of movement. He gasped for a breath, frantically searching for the strength to speak.

"Xavier?" The sound was nothing more than a suspiration, the breath of an Angel.

"I'm here."

Chapter 16: Home is where the heart is

The first box that Xavier had sent sat in the middle of the living room floor: Oliver's toys bursting out. "Pappy's coming home soon Boody!" Katie watched as Oliver, leaning against the large box, reached for the over-sized Pooh Bear that lay on top of the other toys. He made a sound that Elizabeth thought was a giggle.

"He thinks he's two!" she said as Oliver swung the bear awkwardly out of the box and triumphantly plunked it down at his grandmother's feet, his bright blue eyes sparkling, wide with delight. Now ten months old, Oliver, when standing upright, was almost up to Katie's waist. He hadn't quite mastered the art of unaided walking and would mutter protests when he realized he couldn't leave the room with the ease and grace that everyone he saw could; crawling and stair-climbing had been mastered effortlessly since moving in to his grandma's house in Brandon though, as had cupboard opening and fragile object locating.

"Are you sure he's coming back?" Elizabeth watched her daughter, kneeling next to Oliver, carefully pulling toys from the box. Since being released from hospital after the first session of chemotherapy, Elizabeth had detected an air of depressing uncertainty about Katie: she was no longer her lively, sunny self and would evade the subject of Xavier's return when probed. Elizabeth guessed that there were some convoluted problems between the two of them, but was puzzled as to why her daughter wasn't being completely open with her as she had always been in the past. Had it not been for her Grandson's constant demand for attention, she may have had time to dwell on this enigma.

"I don't know Mam." Avoiding her mother's stare, she handed a small, red and yellow and green plastic trumpet to Oliver – a toy that he had loved watching his father animatedly play with. Oliver reached for it immediately with a pudgy pink arm and in doing so momentarily lost his balance as he leant against the cardboard box. Katie chuckled as her son hurriedly made the decision to hold onto the top edge of the box with two hands and then lower himself to a sitting position before attempting to reach for the trumpet. Clutching his toy with both hands, Oliver looked up at Katie and began babbling, his tongue and lips desperately trying to form consonants. He turned his head to the doorway behind Katie and stared into the darkness beyond. The music of Mozart's *Eine kleine Nachtmusik* began again (the CD on repeat for the benefit of Oliver's young, developing mind).

The wind had picked up considerably since teatime; behind the dark green velvet curtains it began throwing heavy raindrops against the sliding glass doors that led out to the small back garden. The living room was comfortingly warm and yet Katie felt a coldness in the room. Her knees ached; using the armrest of the couch, she pulled herself up. Oliver protested; Katie groaned as she picked her son up and sat down next to her mother.

"Here, have some supper Boody!" She lifted her sweatshirt and offered Oliver a nipple. As he suckled, his eyelids began to flutter. "Sometimes I think he'll never be weaned," Katie, keeping her head down, tried to pry the trumpet from Oliver's tight grip as she spoke. "Listen to that wind!" The tree at the edge of the patio sounded as though it was moaning as the wind pulled it this way and that way, its branches slapping together noisily. Katie thought back to the first few weeks in Fort Lauderdale, to the evenings she had spent on the balcony trying to communicate with Xavier, invariably with a beer in his hand and chain smoking: "Keep your voice down Stupid! You really don't care about anyone but yourself do you?" She was fuming: she hated his silence, this sacred cave he withdrew into, defended by select quotes from *Men are from Mars, Women are from Venus*, usually followed by a sanctimonious little laugh. This is how relationships went, he would say, this is how all husbands behaved. Discussion was futile! The more heuristic she became, the further he withdrew, becoming more and more irate until his eyes would squint and glower resolutely straight ahead and his whole body would go taut and begin to quiver as further demands ensued. "You've had enough Xav! Listen to me!" her voice rasping as she desperately tried to reach her husband. One evening, coming home late from a rare and pleasurable shopping spree and finding Xavier halfway though a case of beer, Katie had begun emptying the remaining cans into the kitchen sink. Coming in from the balcony for a fresh drink, Xavier had sworn at her, pushed her aside and grabbed the three beers that were left and stormed back outside pulling the sliding glass door closed with a loud 'wham!' Katie had fallen asleep that night crying, prayers repeating over and over in her head.

Oliver opened his eyes.

"Katie, it's Xavier." Elizabeth treaded softly into the living room. "Did he wake up? Oh, hello Oliver." Her grandson smiled up at her and cooed for a moment before turning his attention to his mother's nipple. Katie painstakingly uprooted herself from the sofa, and with Oliver unremittingly suckling at her breast, went to the phone.

"Thanks Mam," she called as she sat down on the antique, green felt covered piano stool next to the telephone table and picked up the receiver. Xavier waited anxiously for her to speak. "Hello?"

"Katie, I'm coming back at the end of next month. I've handed my notice in and I've put ads in the newspaper for all our stuff and the Jeep. They need me to work until the twenty-fifth. I'll leave after that." His voice was effervescent. Katie looked down at Oliver: his eyes were closed; his lips still. "I got an e…"

"Xav, Can you hang on for a sec?" After placing the receiver on the table, she swapped Oliver into her right arm and pulled her sweatshirt back down. "Boody's so tired. He was up all last night teething. I gave him some Tylenol earlier and I think it's knocked him out! I'm sorry, what were you saying?"

"I'm coming back to Durham." Xavier's voice was quieter.

"What about California? What about your space?" She was being reluctantly defensive. Self-preservation had been her guiding strength after all of Xavier's egregious proclamations of uncertainty about the future: she had realized, since returning to England, that her husband could no longer be depended on for emotional support and had subsequently found within herself a sense of independence and self-worth. Katie knew in her heart that Xavier would always be special to her but had relinquished her clamoring for him. She had become strong again.

"I miss you Katie."

Biting her top lip angrily, Katie tried to arrest the softening she felt inside. She sensed that there was something he wasn't saying, something that he was trying to dig out but couldn't.

"I feel so empty without you and Boody."

Katie heard herself screaming: a glass shattering scream that reverberated throughout the depths of space. She tried to focus her thoughts.

"Are you drunk?" She snapped herself back from the brink.

"I'm tiddly, that's not it! I can see things clearly now. I've been reading this book on Zen and it's made me realize that I was just clouding my own mind with problems. It wasn't you at all! I'm sorry Katie. Please forgive me!"

Katie looked up at the faux Victorian plastered ceiling and breathed in deeply. She felt the downy hairs on her forearms rising up beneath the Sahara restaurant sweatshirt. Although fatigued from the unabating sleep-interrupted nights and exhausting days spent monitoring Oliver's every move, tidying up after the little hobbit constantly and worrying about her mother's condition, Katie's mind began racing. He's done this so many times before, she thought, it's just loneliness that he's feeling; he'll change his mind again soon.

"I got an email from Angela on Friday."

The mention of this name snapped Katie's mind to attention.

"She's leaving Newcastle next week and going to work on a cruise ship for at least six months. I haven't written back to her."

Katie set her teeth, her whole body tightening.

Angela had been Xavier's first fiancée back in his hedonistic modeling days, a girl Katie had questioned Xavier about many times, especially recently since their holiday in England during the summer. Coordinating travel plans with Xavier's parents who were in the process of moving from Northern Cyprus to Zimbabwe, Xavier, Katie and their four month old baby met up with the excited grand parents who were to meet their grandson for the first time. The five of them spent ten days in Aldeburgh on the Suffolk coast in a picturesque seafront cottage. Katie, visiting Suffolk for the first time, was entranced by the tiny village: its quaint narrow streets hung with antique signs advertising 'Fish and Chips', 'Public House', 'Green grocers', 'Fishmongers'; lines of hungry tourists waiting for the freshest fish and chips Katie had ever tasted or ice-cream cones piled unfeasibly high; families sitting at round, wrought iron tables outside the pubs enjoying the sunshine and refreshing sea air. The Lewis' had spent many summer breaks in Aldeburgh (once the home of Lawrence VandePost and the subject of countless well-known landscape paintings and poems) as Albert's parents and youngest sister had lived in villages close by for many years.

Katie, during holiday, watched sadly as her husband (against Doctor's orders) mixed his Prozac with beer every day, going off to the pub in the afternoon to get drunk by himself, leaving her to watch Oliver and to be quizzed by

Albert and Jodie; quizzed about such things as motherhood, the upcoming move from Burlingame to Fort Lauderdale, the extensive maternity leave offered by United Airlines, but never Xavier's drinking or obvious depression. Katie had always wondered why it was that Xavier had turned out so utterly contrasted to his parents; so uncompassionate and hurtful. Denzil appeared to her to be the same way. Visiting Albert's mother and sister – in oddly subdued and removed family reunions, Katie thought, although she was not surprised – Katie again questioned how it could be that Xavier had turned out so distinctly different to his entire family: the matriarchal Grandma Lewis, now eighty-seven years old, was proper to the extreme; where had Albert and Jodie gone wrong with their parenting?

Leaving Suffolk, Katie hoped that the ambience of the remainder of the holiday, to be spent in Durham, would be improved by the reuniting of Xavier and his old friends. A week passed however, with no real improvement, and then one afternoon, out of the blue, Xavier told Katie that he was going for a 'boys' night out'. Intuitively suspecting a deception, Katie and an old school friend went into town to find out just what Xavier was up to. Durham City center was built around a small area and so it was inevitable that she'd ferret him out at some point during the night. Within a couple of hours, she was watching, her heart burning, as her husband, smiling and laughing, talked to a tall, beautiful girl.

"Fucking bastard! Leave him Katie! What a shit-head! I wouldn't put up with it." Katie's friend tried to be empathetic. They followed as Xavier and the tall girl left the nightclub. Katie pushed irascibly into the people climbing the stairs to the club. Finally outside, ignoring Xavier, Katie walked briskly up to the taxi that the stunning girl with long, flowing, dark hair was about to step into.

"Hello, I'm Xavier's wife. Who are you?" She asked firmly, her voice quavering ever so slightly.

"I'm sorry. Goodnight Xav." The tall stranger glanced at her for an instant, a look in her deep brown eyes that made Katie want to break into tears: there was no fear, no happiness, no anxiety in her eyes. It was more of a solemnity, a sorrow that spoke volumes; spoke of a knowing, a realization that she was mixed up in the same situation that her own father had got himself into five years earlier, shortly before her parents had divorced. She glanced quickly at Xavier, a faint smile coming to her lips, then stepped into the taxi, pulled the door shut and was gone.

"Who was that?" Katie grabbed Xavier's arm. Tears streamed from her eyes.

"I was just saying goodnight. That's Angela. Get off me!" He was drunk and in a rage. Breaking free of Katie's grip, he turned suddenly, dodged around a taxi that was pulling up and ran off up the street. Katie followed him. It was drizzling lightly, the wet road glistening romantically with the reflections of the street lights and so Katie's 'going out' shoes didn't provide much traction. There weren't that many people out either, as it was mid-week, and so Xavier was quickly gone.

"Don't come back!" Katie screamed after him as she came to a halt, her face wet with rain and tears.

Four hours later, repentant and dejected, a bedraggled Xavier stood below the bedroom window, the pieces of gravel bouncing of the glass with a soft 'ping'. He hadn't had enough money to get a taxi all the way back from Angela's house in Lanchester (halfway to Newcastle) and so had walked the remaining three miles from Nevilles Cross, where the 'stingy bastard' taxi driver (as Xavier had called him after he had driven off) had dropped him, claiming he had another pick-up to make. Xavier and Angela had talked for ages about the future: he saying that the passion they had felt a decade earlier was reason enough to make another go of it; she saying that she couldn't move backwards, that she had to move on; they were good friends, they always had been and always would be, but that was all.

"I thought that I might still be in love with her. I thought that was why I was unhappy. I don't love her anymore Katie, but I had to make sure."

Katie studied her husband, a pathetic figure hunched over on the sofa with his head in his hands, his fine, short hair tousled unattractively. As she listened to him, she felt the first thorns of indifference pierce her heart. His speech was slurred, now mostly from fatigue. "I don't love her Katie!" Xavier raised his head and looked directly at her. Unable to gather the strength to feign any emotion at this moment, least of all remorse, his bloodshot eyes burned with anger. Katie rose silently and left the room.

"Are you coming back because she's left you?" Her voice emotionless, Katie guilefully dropped a lure.

There was silence. Katie yawned.

"She's neither the problem nor the answer. She was dust that I let cloud my mirror. Xavier impressed himself whenever he 'oh, so casually' dropped in a Zen phrase to a conversation. "I don't care that she's leaving. Why should I? I'm sorry Katie. I'm so sorry! I love you." The last three words were almost whispered.

"Are you alright Katie?" Elizabeth, peeking around the living room door saw her daughter, tears streaming from her eyes, cradling the contented, sleeping baby, a wet patch on Oliver's gray romper suit. "Let me put him in bed for you."

"I'm fine Mam." Katie looked at her mother – her poor, dying mother – and all of a sudden felt the urge to scream, to cry out to God and tell him to stop killing her. She closed her eyes for a moment. "I'll call you next week Xav. God bless. I love you." Katie replaced the receiver and sniffled. "He's coming back." Smiling painfully as she wiped her eyes, she longed for a great big hug, to be embraced tightly, to be held the way she held Oliver, to feel that love. Elizabeth, much weaker than ever before, (her hair thinning markedly too) no longer had the strength to squeeze the breath out of her daughter as she had done the previous year. After putting Oliver into his crib, Katie, with a feeling of resignation and great fatigue lumbered back down stairs. Elizabeth was standing in the bay window to the left of the front door, her enervated figure reflected off the darkness beyond the small lawn outside. The wind had died down and there was a calming silence in the house that Katie rarely experienced these days.

"Look Katie! It's snowing!" The porch light illuminated the first delicate snowflakes of the winter as they fell gently, silently. Katie put both arms around her mother's waist, and laying her head on her bosom, wept quietly.

Chapter 17: Freedom (opus one)

'I am proud and free. I am an African.' A smile – no more than a narrowing of the eyes and a tightening of the muscles around the mouth – crossed Denzil's face. He carefully closed the heavy photo album, rested his hands on the front cover and focused his eyes on the patterns that his fingers and their shadows created on the gray vinyl. His wedding ring glinted brightly like a golden, autumn, crescent moon. Using his thumb, he rolled it around his finger, his mind drifting away on the whiskey. The skin covering his knuckles was bunched up and formed tiny, smiling faces; each of them had their own unique, lively and comical character. Like his mother's hands, Denzil's were long and slender; the skin tender and smooth; his nails perfectly shaped and well kept. He recalled the hours he had spent in front of the piano mastering fingering techniques in Nhyaesu; these same hands running up and down the keys of the grand piano in the bright, spacious living room, practicing scales under the patient supervision of Mrs. Lewis, piano teacher and mother. No one could have imagined that those gentle hands would become so powerful and destructive.

"You've broken his jaw!" The coach of the Brandon Boxing Club, wearing the obligatory Adidas sweat suit that all trainers wore to look like they meant business, on his knees beside the unconscious body of Denzil's sparring partner, looked up at him in disbelief. Denzil towered over him, his head seemingly too small (even with the large 'Afro') perched on top of his huge upper body. At nineteen years of age and after only four months of boxing training, Denzil, his body already massively developed from four years of extreme weight-lifting and three more years of competitive athletics, had the strength and coordination required for a great future in boxing, but looking down at the twisted and motionless body on the mat, blood trailing from the side of the young man's mouth, Denzil silently removed his gloves and stepped out of the ring and never returned.

Denzil closed his eyes and immediately felt the earth begin to shudder: not the same tremors as the deadly earthquake and the numerous aftershocks he'd experienced as he sat at his desk in the Aviansa corporate office in the center of San Salvador shortly after Nina and Rebecca had left for England produced, this was a tighter, more urgent shudder. He quickly gripped the arms of the wicker chair and clenched his jaw. The shuddering gradually began to subside. 'I am proud and free. I am an African!' his mind reaffirmed his strength. Reaching cautiously for the whiskey bottle, he brought it to his lips and took a long draught. Swallowing hard, he thought back to the day he met his father's brother – his uncle, the Colonel.

A puzzled Albert had welcomed the stranger in. Denzil, glancing at his mother, had noticed the look of utter shock on her face as the oddly sheepish imposing African entered the living room. The very blood in her face seemed to drain instantly. Her mouth opened slightly as though she was gasping for air.

"Jodie, this is Colonel Acheompong. He says he knows you and Denzil." It took Albert a few more moments before the name registered. "I'll get some drinks," he said excusing himself after it had finally clicked.

"Ernest, how on earth did you find us?"

Denzil, unable to take his eyes off this stranger, heard an unexpected friendliness and familiarity in his mother's voice and pictured her with a huge smile stretched across her face.

"Dr. Amu called me to let me know that you and Denzil were in Accra for a few days. He is still a close friend." The Colonel moved forward hesitantly and for the first time since he'd entered the room took his eyes off Jodie and looked directly at Denzil; his eyes piercing and authoritative. "I am your uncle," he said in response to the look on Denzil's face.

Jodie was now standing and invited him to join the three of them. Xavier was also standing, sporting a bemused look, complete with a fatuous grin, corroborated by his wavy, blonde hair.

A member of the Ga tribe of southern Ghana who were typically tall and handsome, Colonel Acheompong stood well over six feet; an impressive figure with broad shoulders and shaven head wearing a dark gray suit. He walked over to Denzil purposefully. Denzil, breathing hard as the anxiety built up quickly, shook his uncle's large hand, imagining his father standing before him. "It's good to finally meet you, a grown man Denzil." Although smiling, his voice was deep and somber.

Jodie had thrown away all the photos of her first husband and so Denzil had only a rough picture in his mind of his father painted by vague descriptions his mother had given him. This man standing in front of him was much more dignified and impressive than the image he had created.

In the kitchen, Albert stayed within earshot.

"Please sit down Ernest," Jodie motioned to an armchair. The University guesthouse in Legon, near Accra, that Albert had booked for a week was furnished in a traditional, colonial fashion with wicker chairs and tables, hand-carved Ashanti stools and the odd imported European piece such as the cushioned armchair to which Jodie was motioning. Denzil sat down on a stool to his uncle's left. He'd barely taken his eyes off the Colonel since he'd entered the room; this long-lost relative, a man whose face seemed so foreign and yet so familiar, fascinated him.

"You're a fine man Denzil. Your mother has raised you well."

"With the help of my father, "Denzil responded immediately.

Albert was still in the kitchen allowing time for the reunion to progress without any uneasiness.

"It is true. My brother did many wrong things. I know that he was sorry for leaving you and your mother."

"I left him!" Jodie retorted. "What he did was a terrible thing: stealing Denzil from me!" She was still standing. There was no smile on her face.

"Yes, I know, Mrs. Lewis..." Colonel Acheompong looked up as Albert entered the room carrying a tray of glasses filled with ice and lemonade. Waiting until everyone had a drink, the Colonel stood up and holding his glass high made a toast. "To Professor and Mrs. Lewis, for the commendable job they have done raising this fine young man. Continue to be proud and free Denzil. You are an African man!" He looked at his nephew, still seated, and smiled as he took a drink.

Denzil opened the photo album again and thumbed to the pages that contained the photographs taken at this first meeting. The album was a photographic record of the holiday the family had spent in Ghana in nineteen ninety-one; Albert had been back many times, monitoring the renovation projects being funded by CEDECOM and UNESCO, but this three week holiday was the only time the Lewis' had been back to the boys' homeland as a family. Page after page of blissful memories; of the rediscovery of freedom; of awakening lay upon Denzil's lap. A loose photograph of Rebecca, sitting in a red and green child's wheelbarrow, fell out as Denzil turned a page. His daughter's innocent, grinning face lit up his heart. He gazed deep into her light brown eyes. With a myriad of colors, the dusk had begun painting a magnificent sunset over the dormant volcanoes to the west of the city; the declivitous slopes awash with hues of orange and red were speckled here and there with tiny twinkling lights. Picking up the photograph, Denzil kissed Rebecca's image and slid it into his shirt pocket. Looking out across Cuscatlan – a large suburb to the east of San Salvador – from the rooftop terrace of his simple apartment, a delicious, warm breeze blowing down from mountains to the south, Denzil began to feel a tranquility in his heart that he'd noticed many months ago had disappeared. Even the birth of his son hadn't been able to erase the doubt in his mind that the smiles he wore and the laughter that erupted from his mouth every now and then were spurious.

Nina had left San Salvador for Birmingham, England, taking Rebecca away from him almost eleven months earlier: forty-three weeks; three hundred days that Denzil had counted off on his calendar each morning as he sat down in his cubicle at the Aviansa corporate offices in the city center. The walls of this eight feet square partitioned booth were lined with photographs of his daughter and pictures she'd drawn for him in crayon on white sheets of printer paper: there was a picture of a spider in the middle of a web; a collection of odd looking Dalmatians of varying sizes – drawn after she's watched the film *101 Dalmatians*; a collection of scribbles and attempts at writing in English – 'I love you DADDY' was emblazoned across one sheet in five different colors. Whenever Nina and Rebecca had come to visit him at work, Rebecca would surprise her father by peeking around the corner of his booth, laughing and screeching loudly like a hyena the moment they made eye contact.

The feeling of tranquility had left him. 'Life goes on like this, onwards until we die!' Denzil shut his eyes and wept tears of hurt that slashed his cheeks like hateful daggers. 'It's not my fault that I didn't love you.' His mind boiled. 'You can't keep her from me!' The sky was dark, and the breeze, no longer delicious, carried a rancid smell of rot and putrefaction. Denzil took the half-empty bottle of whiskey with him down the exterior, whitewashed concrete staircase and finished it sitting in the almost completely bare living room watching large bottomed Hispanic women dancing provocatively on some late-night television show.

Xavier sucked at his cigarette. His eyes were closed, keeping him safely hidden from his tormentor. He remembered his fear as a child, hiding in the laundry basket in the bathroom, his terror and the rank odor of sweaty clothes bringing him to the verge of vomiting, watching his father through the thin slats in the wicker as he walked down the hallway – the same hallway the mysterious shadowy ghost that Xavier had seen walk down many times through the glass brick wall that separated the hallway from the bedroom he and Denzil shared – towards the bathroom, disappearing into the bedroom for a minute; remembered wishing he would suffocate amongst the dirty laundry just so that his mother would be angry at his father for causing his death (oh how his father would be sorry then!) and everyone would cry because he was dead; vividly recalled catching a glimpse of the brown leather slipper his father was carrying; feeling the basket jounce as the circular lid was pulled off and shutting his eyes tight to keep himself safe and unseen; hearing the anger in his father's voice as he dragged him up by his arm through the sweaty laundry.

"Are you drunk?" Katie asked again.

The cold of the North Eastern, late spring night stung his nostrils as he inhaled. He had been sober for the entire week preceding Elizabeth's funeral and was now catching up.

"I can't talk to you when you're drunk!"

"Well, leave me alone then!" Xavier's head began to spin: he opened his eyes. Katie, standing over him, was once again ruining a lovely buzz. He chugged the last of his beer, crushed the can and opened a fresh one, dropping the crumpled tin onto the pile of empties – it was cold enough outdoors to keep what was left of the two four-packs he'd bought at the Spa earlier chilled. "I should have stayed in America!" he said quietly, refusing to let himself look at Katie. He knew how much pain she was in; knew how much he was hurting her; wished he could hold her and comfort her. Perhaps if, as a child growing up, he had experienced that closeness, that love, he may have been able to bring himself to reach out for her; but unfortunately, he was empty.

"What do you mean by that? Do you want to be single? I don't care if you do, Xavier. Leave now if you want to run away from your responsibilities, Oliver and I will be alright." Katie waited for some kind of response, any kind of response from her husband.

Xavier put the can to his lips, sadly accepting that his buzz was lost and drank for no other reason than there was beer left to ingest.

"I want to understand why it is that I drink. I see what it's doing to my life, but I don't want to stop. My wife needs me more than ever now and I can't even touch her." Xavier had just finished recounting to the therapist the

155

holiday that he, Katie and Oliver had been on to Tenerife just before Elizabeth's death: Katie's father, against Katie's wishes, had booked the flights and hotel, and at the insistence of Elizabeth, hospitalized for her third session of chemotherapy, the three of them had traveled to Puerto de la Cruz and spent a restless week with Katie's multi-millionaire Spanish father. The two-week holiday was cut short however, and Xavier had celebrated his thirty-first birthday traveling back to Durham with Katie and Oliver following a phone call from Katie's twin brother Alex to say that their mother was dying. Stopping at a service station on the A1(M) just south of Doncaster at eight fifteen in the evening so that Katie could call Dryburn Hospital to check on her mother, and so that Xavier, having driven non-stop since leaving the rental car office at Gatwick airport, could stretch his legs, Xavier, obstinately leaning against the car, watched his wife break down as she received the news; watched, callously refusing to let himself go to her, to hold her, as she lent her head against the glass side panel of the phone box and wept

"All I wanted to do then was to get a beer", he continued. "I can see that it's destroying my life but when I drink," he paused for a moment, lowered his head and then scratched his cheek. His eyes darted about as though charged with electricity. "I feel so much less pain. Sometimes, I even feel alive again!"

The therapist, a kind-faced lady in her fifties with long gray hair tied back in a ponytail, scribbled in her white, ruled A4 notebook. She studied him carefully for a moment.

"Do you want to continue like this? Drinking and feeling unhappy I mean."

Xavier looked up. Through the window behind the therapist, Xavier saw rooftops bathed in sunlight. He wished he were outside, out of this damp shadowy room, feeling the warmth of the sun. But here he was and this was going to help. He glanced around the room taking in some of the titles of the books on the IKEA bought bookcase below the window; 'I bet if I read all those books I could do her job,' he said to himself. The therapist missed the smile that washed over Xavier's face as he spotted Benjamin Hoff's *The Te of Piglet* and *The Tao of Pooh*, two books he had bought at the Barnes and Noble bookstore on Haight Street in San Francisco; books he had enjoyed reading to baby Oliver as he slept. There was a tall, healthy looking yucca plant in an ornate, red clay pot to the left of the bookcase and a bronzy, brushed chrome waste-paper bucket on the other side. Some sheets from the therapist's notebook were sticking out, standing at a slight angle, folded length-ways. Three framed certificates were on the wall above the yucca: the Doctor's full name was Vivien Marigold Otley. Was this Stuart's mother he wondered? She was about the right age. Would she tell her son about the private, intimate problems of Xavier Lewis? Would this get back to all of his friends? Realizing he was letting his mind wander, Xavier breathed in deeply,

157

coughing as some saliva hit the back of his throat. He leaned forward and picked up the glass from the low coffee table (also from IKEA) that was between Dr. Otley and himself and took a sip of water.

"I want to be a good father and husband." He carefully placed the glass down, sat back in the armchair, paused and turned his hands, which were now resting on the armrests of the deep and comfortable, dark green leather chair, to look at his fingernails: he shrewdly hid them in slack fists. "I feel as though I have no valid reasons to feel depressed, especially compared to everything my wife has been through. And now I need to help her with her grieving process. I tell myself that my pain can't be anywhere near as intense as hers."

"Do you feel as though your problems are invalidated?"

"Yes", Xavier replied without hesitation.

Doctor Vivien Otley wrote for what seemed to Xavier to be a little too long and then looking up at Xavier, spoke suddenly. "That'll be all for this week."

Shaking his hand, she thanked him and he left her damp, shadowy office and headed straight for the 'Swan and three Signets' pub across the road.

Denzil reached for the light switch. The poster of the Airbus A320 on the wall next to the bedroom door was illuminated by the orange glow of the streetlamp across the road from his apartment; the thin brown curtains were about as effective as paper. With the way the shadows lay

158

across the wall, the aircraft appeared to be in motion, the clouds below it undulating. He could hear the soft breathing of his lover and his child, almost following the same rhythm.

'To fly away silently across the seas,

to worlds to which we've never been,

except for maybe on journeys in our minds,

where eventually our freedom we find."

Denzil lay down and closed his eyes, shutting out the darkness.

Chapter 18: July 1999

Jodie let out a sigh of relief as the British Midland's London-Newcastle flight came to a complete stop with a quick lurch. She let go of Albert's hand and raised the window blind; painfully bright sunlight streamed in. As her eyes adjusted to the sudden brightness, Jodie watched the familiar terminal come into focus, and for a brief moment thought she could see Xavier and Katie, with Oliver in her arms, watching the aircraft through the wall of glass as the jetway was carefully maneuvered into place against the front door.

"…We're at Newcastle airport. We were expecting to see you here. Did you get our email Xavier?" His father's voice was almost frightening. He couldn't remember answering the phone or what was first said. 'Fuck! What time is it?' He looked around for a clock that worked. The house was dead silent.

"No Dad, I didn't. When did you get in?" 'I must still be drunk,' he thought. 'Wake up!'

"About an hour ago. We'll get the Metro to Newcastle and then catch a train to Durham. Will you be able to meet us at the station? We should be there by ten."

"Sure."

"How are Katie and Oliver?" Albert was puzzled. "Xavier's at the house," he said angrily to Jodie who was leaning against the luggage-laden trolley yawning.

"Fine. She must have gone out with Oliver."

"Oh, well we can't wait to see you all."

Denzil opened his eyes confidently: no hangover this morning. He felt peculiar waking up without that horrid, unmerciful pounding in his head. The daylight slashed through the gap between the thin handmade curtains – curtains Nina's mother had made for the house in San Pedro Sula. He had been left with very little when Nina and Rebecca left. His mother-in-law had traveled from Honduras with one of Nina's cousins in an battered, green Toyota pick-up to help Nina pack up everything that had been given to the newly weds as wedding gifts, house-warming presents, Christmas presents, anything given to them as a couple. When Nina and her mother left, taking with them the only treasure he had – his beautiful, brown-eyed daughter Rebecca – he had cried for what seemed like an eternity; this had truly felt like the eternity of Hell as Joyce described in *Portrait of an artist as a young man.* The curtains had been overlooked. Rubbing the sleep that was crusted to his eyelashes, he pulled apart the curtains.

Using his elbow to prop himself up, he lifted his muscular upper body off the musty smelling mattress that Sophia had brought with her when she moved in, and looked out at the quiet street. Across the narrow street, next to the bus stop, the old, bent Indian woman who came there every day had set up her stall already and was busy arranging a variety of fruit in open boxes. She always had a serenity about her, an aura of enlightenment, as though she had been left over from the fall of the Mayans, the sole remaining survivor of the mysterious blight that either killed off or drove out the Mayans from what is now El Salvador. Denzil looked up at the sky. Today, this bright blue-sky day, was going to be a wonderful day. As he looked around the room, he saw his infant son, Ben sleeping soundly in the ornate, hand-made wooden crib he had bought from the local artisans' market. Sophia had been asleep when he had come to bed, there had been no lovemaking earlier in the evening and so there was bound to be some this morning. Ignoring all the dangers, the medical and social advice, and even though the local Doctor knew him too well, Denzil was still a devout onanist. Hearing the soft pads of his lover's feet on the cool, cream painted concrete floor, Denzil turned to see Sophia, her long black hair hanging, still wet, over one shoulder, a faded seashell printed towel wrapped bashfully around her full figure, walking down the hall from the bathroom, the towel only just managing to keep her decent. She glanced at her sleeping child and, satisfied that he was

162

fast asleep, pulled the sheet from the foot of the bed and slipped in next to Denzil, dropping the towel on the floor. Denzil closed his eyes and dreamed of Ghana, of innocence, of utopia. He found peace in his onanism.

Albert fidgeted on the wrought iron bench outside Durham railway station. He could hear a car approaching, struggling up the steep hill that led to the station. He turned again to look at the clock hanging above the platform. He huffed as a white Ford Escort appeared from around the bend. Beside him, Jodie was nodding off in the warm sunshine. 'Where on earth could he be?' Albert cleared his throat. The sky was a translucent blue with a few small, high, white clouds. The smell of diesel was oddly reassuring.

"Here he is now dear!"

Jodie, startled, lifted her head and saw a blue Volvo pulling up a few feet away. As Xavier stepped out she recognized the car as Elizabeth's reliable old Volvo; the car Elizabeth had bought from Katie the day before Katie and Xavier left for America. Albert was rearranging the suitcases and bags.

"Hello Xavier," he said opening his arms to greet a very wan looking Xavier. Jodie lifted herself up and stiffly walked towards her son.

"How was the trip? I bet you're exhausted." Xavier, having briefly hugged his father, embraced Jodie a little more affectionately.

Albert began carrying the luggage to the car. "It was okay; very long though. We left Bulawayo at seven o'clock yesterday morning!"

The drive to Brandon was a strain for Xavier: he knew his parents could smell the alcohol on his breath; knew they wanted to see everything perfect; knew he had let them down; wished he could close his eyes and be transported away from this mess.

"We'd like to take some flowers to the cemetery at some point. Would you be able to run us out there one day Katie?" Albert found himself talking to his daughter-in-law so that he didn't have to look at Xavier. Jodie was playing as best she could with Oliver on the patio, Oliver laughing vivaciously as he played with an inflatable yellow hammer. Albert smiled as he watched Jodie floundering with a disposable camera she'd bought in W.H. Smith's whilst waiting in Newcastle's Central station for the train to Durham, attempting to decipher the instructions. Katie was holding up pretty well, he thought, she certainly appeared to be in a better state than Xavier was.

"Of course, any time will be fine. We'll pick you up from Claudia's. Do you need me to take you anywhere else?"

"No, we'll be fine with the trains and buses. We're going to see an old colleague of mine in Newcastle on Thursday, but we'll take the train. Thank you for offering though. Won't you be using the car to get to work Xavier?" Albert reluctantly turned to look at his son. Xavier blinked a couple of times, rubbed one bloodshot eye and then the other with his sweaty hands before clearing his throat to speak.

"I've taken this week off."

"Oh, you shouldn't have done that. Anyway, how is the restaurant? We'll have to go for dinner one evening."

"The food's not that good. There are lots of places better," Xavier continued lying.

Dropping the subject, Albert got up from the sofa, stretched his arms out with a low, satisfied groan and bringing them back in walked to the open sliding glass door. The summer air was intoxicatingly fresh and clean, laden with the scents of lavender and fresh hay. Oliver, making eye contact with his grandfather, began making his way unsteadily towards him.

"He's growing so fast. I wish we all lived closer to one another." Oliver was the only one who heard him speak, raising his eyebrows in response.

"Are you ready for some lunch?" Katie joined Albert in the doorway, and seeing the slightly uneven patio stone in front of her son, stooped down just in time to rescue a stumbling Oliver from a minor fall.

"He isn't growing out of it", Jodie fastidiously, so that ironing wouldn't be necessary again, folded her mauve wool cardigan and placed it in the second drawer of the antique, dark oak armoire and gingerly pushed the

165

stubborn drawer closed. On the wall to her left, an oil painting of a Matador resplendent in victory, one foot resting on the carcass of the defeated bull wobbled precariously; Jodie reached out her arm in anticipation. The painting didn't fall. "In seven years, nothing has changed!" She paused. "Albert?" Turning her head, she looked towards Albert who was sitting in one of two well-worn, dark red corduroy covered armchairs that were by the window. His eyes were closed; his head bowed. Jodie softly walked over and sat down in the other armchair – equally red and worn and comfortable – on the opposite side of a small whitewashed wicker coffee table that completed the set. She removed the woolen tea-cozy from the teapot, poured herself a second cup of tea and with the dainty china at her lips, looked across the street to the pink house on the end of the terrace opposite.

192 Cragpath had been the Lewis' third home in Durham, for two years from nineteen eighty-six. Walking around the Victorian, three story end-terrace house at the top of a hill overlooking the Durham city center with it's Cathedral and Castle perched upon another hill-top (surrounded on three sides by the River Wear), Jodie had imagined this house to be her dream home, the one she would grow old enjoying life in, spending sunny afternoons tending the small, sloping garden from which one had an awe-inspiring view of the Cathedral and Castle, teaching her piano students in the high-ceilinged, wood

floored living room with its great bay window with the same wonderful view as from the garden and kitchen downstairs and the master bedroom upstairs. It had been an easy sale for the real-estate agent. Whispering to Albert they stood outside the front door that one had to step down to reach (the pavement level having been raised for some unknown reason many years before), Jodie had felt excitement, exhilaration coursing through her veins: she felt like a teenager getting ready for her first date. Within two weeks, they had moved in.

Three nights later, the first beer bottle smashed through the street level bathroom window. The entire terrace of three story houses on the west side of Cragpath, overlooking Durham Cathedral, was built on the steeply sloping hillside with their middle floor at street level. The price the Lewis' (and the two owners before them) paid for only having neighbors on one side was that where a house had once stood – the terrace of houses in years gone by, before the dual-carriageway had sliced through, had continued on and up the next hill known as Gilesgate bank – a fairly new bus shelter with large glass panels had been erected. Also, being at the top of a hill meant that at the weekend, late night revelers, having reached the summit after an exhausting hike would rest, noisily, in the bus shelter. The glass panels were shattered on a regular basis by drunken juvenile delinquents. When there was no glass left to smash, the small window of a tiny bathroom of the 'pink house' (as everyone knew it) was targeted. A few yards further on from the bus stop was a pedestrian bridge that led across the dual carriage-way to Gilesgate bank making for an easy get-away for the vandals (or 'yobos' as Jodie dubbed them).

Eighteen months after they moved into 192 Cragpath, the Lewis' packed up and left the house of nightmares. On the opposite side of the street, mid-terrace, Claudia Giovanni had lived in peace for many years. A good friend the Lewis' had made soon after moving into the pink house (Denzil, at the time working for West Midlands Police Force, coming home at the weekends, had enjoyed a brief relationship with the pretty daughter), Claudia ran her house as a busy bed and breakfast. It was the window of 'The Spanish Room' on the second floor that Jodie was now looking out of. She felt an apprehension rising inside her as she recalled the innumerable nights that she had lain in bed, in that pink house of horrors, every muscle in her body taut, eyes wide open, listening to the rambunctious voices of the yobos, thick with the easily recognizable North Eastern accent; waiting for the screams of delight as glass shattered in a cacophony of wild abandon. Albert, all of a sudden stirred in his slumber – a murmuring that Jodie had become accustomed to. Lost in her reflections, she didn't hear the knock at the door and the faint voice calling, "Telephone."

Her tone was injured and conspiratorial. "Why won't you stop living in a dream Xav? You're thirty-one; you have a son who needs a responsible father. You're not a child any more!" Xavier's conscious mind was tucked snuggly away in its secret cave, enjoying the tranquility and serenity as Katie made her futile attempts to talk some sense into her husband. "You need a job to take care of Oliver. You're never going to be a *Pop Star!*" With this last sentence, her voice became soft; full of empathy. "You have to work to make money." Katie reached out and took hold of Xavier's arm in a gesture of tenderness. The unexpected gentleness of her touch startled Xavier enough to make him turn to look at Katie sitting next to him on the sofa. He was about to smile, about to break, but vaguely recalled Katie saying something about his musical ambitions. He stared at her blankly for a moment and then, pulling his arm free of Katie's soft hold, got up suddenly and went into the kitchen.

At the end of the previous summer, looking forward to retirement that was only two years away, Elizabeth Selleck had had her entire kitchen renovated. The improvements had been expensive but the sparkling new kitchen had made her final days in the house a pleasure: light gray marble floor tiles; a darker gray granite counter top; an impressive granite double sink below the small window that looked out into the quiet cul-de-sac; fitted white drawers and cupboards, inside two of which were secreted the small fridge and an automatic dishwasher (Katie at first could not remember which doors they were behind and would have to open a couple of cupboards before finding the right one), and the piece-de-resistance, an almost perfectly camouflaged, state-of-the-art flat-topped electric stove – its purpose was merely hinted at if one noted the digital clock and five circular controls (for the hot-plates and the oven). The room, although dazzling was still narrow and cramped. It was tucked away, partially under the stairs along a side wall of the dining room behind sliding half glass doors, as though the builder had remembered at the last moment that the house needed a kitchen. Katie kept the kitchen spotless (as Elizabeth had), going over the granite counter top and stove top with a damp, soapy sponge at the end of every visit making Xavier, an avid chef, reluctant to cook anything for fear of making a mess that Katie would berate him for.

"What's the matter?"
"Nothing!" Xavier's voice was flat. He switched on the kettle, reached into the cupboard above the toaster and took down a red mug with 'Johnson's Shopfitters' printed in white letters around it, scooped one teaspoon of instant coffee and two of sugar into it and turned to his wife who was standing in the doorway. "I can't go on like this Katie! I'm going to stay with Charlie and Georgina."

Xavier, having been unable to get in touch with his parents to inform them of his plan to move out, had decided that there was no time to lose; the tense atmosphere in that small brick house in Brandon was more than he could take. Oliver played quietly outside below high, stationary clouds in his new green turtle-shaped sandpit in the back garden building a city for his collection of Hot Wheels cars to drive around as Xavier packed up his clothes and few possessions upstairs in the front bedroom.

"I'll call my parents and tell them we won't be having dinner with them tomorrow." Xavier wiped a tear from his cheek with the yellow cotton sweater he was holding. The bedroom, left empty once Katie had left home, still smelt musty; Xavier sniffled unintentionally. Still in a daze, Katie was sitting on the edge of her mother's old queen-size bed watching her husband pack. Just then the doorbell rang. Looking out of the window, Xavier saw Charlie's light blue Renault Clio, its paint gleaming in the sunshine, parked on the curve of the cul-de-sac in front of the house. Standing on the 'Welcome' doormat, Xavier's old friend acknowledged Katie with a subtle nod and a muffled hello. Xavier had gone back upstairs and Charlie had an uneasy feeling in his stomach, guilt perhaps, as he stood waiting: Katie (a woman he knew only slightly, most of what he knew had come from Xavier), not saying a word. Oliver was hiding behind Katie, clutching her leg and smiling and peering at this dark-haired man he vaguely recognized.

Upon Xavier's insistence, Katie had befriended Charlie's wife Georgina shortly before Xavier had returned from Florida. Charlie's daughter Danielle was eighteen months older than Oliver and "would be a great girlfriend for Oliver," Xavier had said over and over again. The two mothers had quickly developed a close, 'sisters in arms' friendship (a bond that Charlie furtively despised) and would visit each other's homes regularly swapping tales of relationship woes over lunch or cups of tea and coffee while their children played. Charlie would return home from work to find the two women gossiping in the living room. The conversation would cease as he entered the room and they would both turn to look at him derisively as though he was interrupting an important meeting. Charlie – a tall, dark and handsome man (his father was Portuguese), with the look of a young Elvis about him – and Georgina had met during the late eighties when Georgina was studying at St. Mary's college in Durham. The rock band that Charlie and Xavier and couple of friends had formed a couple of years earlier was well known throughout the colleges of Durham University and had accumulated a sizable fan base. Georgina's friends would drag her out to see the band play at whichever college they were booked at and after turning down the advances of all the other band members, Georgina – an exquisite petite Asian-Irish young student – had accepted Charlie's rose-accompanied request for a date making him the envy of all his friends.

"This is the last bag," Xavier said reaching the bottom of the stairs. Charlie breathed a sigh of relief. "I'll call you tomorrow. Bye Boody." Xavier, trying with all of his might to hold back the tears, leaned down and kissed Oliver on the forehead. "I love you," his voice faltered as he spoke to his son, a puzzled look forming on the boy's pink-cheeked face.

"See you later Katie. Bye Oliver," Charlie said as he left, waving quickly to Oliver who was being restrained from following Xavier to the car.

"Daddy!"

Xavier didn't look back.

Chapter 19: Submission

Oliver was asleep in the pushchair, his head twisted to one side; some of his lunch – a corned beef and potato pasty from Gregg's no doubt, by the looks of the mass of crumbs in his lap – stuck to his cheek. Noticing Xavier's gaze, Katie adjusted Oliver's hat to shield his eyes from the bright sun and brushed the food off his cheek. It was a beautiful autumn day, a light breeze sifting Xavier's hair.

"Are you happy Xav?" There was a hint of tenderness in her voice.

Two and a half months of emptiness spent with friends in pubs and a swelling, soul-draining sadness and Xavier was reaching a breaking point. For a while life at Charlie's house gave Xavier the freedom he enduringly craved: he could come and go as he pleased; stay out until dawn; get as drunk as he wanted (or could); eat only when he wanted to; get out of bed when he felt like it; keep his responsibilities tucked away snuggly in a dark, hard-to-reach recess in the back of his mind. There was only one rule that Georgina and Charlie had asked him to abide by:

no girls back to the house. Social Security payments came every other Thursday and with money from odd jobs here and there – mostly working for friends – Xavier found he could get drunk every night. This was what he wanted, wasn't it? Surely this was the freedom he had been yearning for. He had his own space, his own tiny bedroom with a dusty, roll-down raffia blind, his books and CDs and a mattress on the floor. He missed his son dearly though, missed his smile, his giggles, and Angela was gone too, taking with her some part of Xavier that kept him from being able to feel the love towards Katie that he should have felt. Refusing to be pulled into her snare he forced himself to remain aloof. "I'll change," or "Let's try to make it work" she'd say resolutely when they met each week in the bustling, cobblestoned Market Place so that Oliver could see his father.

"Am I happy?" Xavier turned and looked around the Market Place. No one was looking at the three of them. The steps at the base of the Statue that stood in the center were lined with people, with shirt sleeves rolled up, skirts pulled high revealing pinky white thighs, relaxing in the unusually warm, late-autumn sunshine; there were mothers pushing prams or dragging their protesting youngsters; the odd man in a business suit clutching his mobile phone to his ear; clusters of scruffy youths smoking; no-one paying any attention to him. He scraped his bottom lip with his teeth as he inhaled. The appetizing smell of onions cooking

175

at a burger stand wafted by, carried on a cool, gentle breeze.

"I don't think you are Xav. Let's try to make it work, we can get through this. I promise I'll trust you."

"You say that, but I know in a month it'll be the same as it was Katie! I'm not coming back. If we stay separated Oliver will suffer less. He's already used to me not being there. We'll get back together and then what? He'll hear us fighting all the time; I'll move out again. It's not fair on him." Xavier loathed these meetings; Katie's constant nagging; the crowds. He felt as though the passers-by were listening in on their conversation, judging him: 'look at that man, leaving his family. What a loser! What a stupid, fucking loser!'

The Market Place in Durham was a focal point for the city and the surrounding villages. The restored St. Nicholas' Church, erected in the eighteen hundreds, stood proudly along the north side of the square. There was a pub, 'The Market Tavern' (almost a hundred years older than the Church) that at lunch time attracted civil servants from the City Council offices that occupied a number of buildings on the lower end of Cragpath, no more than two minutes' walk away, who would enjoy a fine traditional pub lunch washed down with a couple of pints of lager or ale. A busy indoor market underneath the seventeenth century City Guildhall buildings drew housewives and the unemployed from near and far; residents of the City and also people from the small mining villages that surrounded the city, who, having traveled in by bus would spend hours ambling around the vendors' stalls that flaunted everything from fresh fish to shoes, and on Fridays and Saturdays a number of vendors would set up their stalls in the Market Place itself around the imposing statue of the third Marquess of Londonderry on his steed. All this created a great deal of noise and bustle in the pedestrianized area that made Xavier twist in his daytime sobriety. He took off his sunglasses to rub his eyes and then replaced them. The Church bells pealed the hour and then, after a short pause, struck one. Oliver, exhausted from a morning of playing with his mother, slept through the ringing.

"Yes, I am happy. I'm not coming back Katie. I'm not." He stroked Oliver's cheek as though making sure all the crumbs were off, mumbled something about next week and left, walking towards Cragpath and the Belmont Hopper bus stop. As the old, dirty bus, dark gray smoke billowing from its exhaust pipe – hardly the mode of transportation that the name suggested, with graffiti scrawled along the sides and back ('Baz luvs Shaz' caught Xavier's eye as he had boarded) – struggled to the brow of the hill, Xavier watched as the pink house came into view. A sickly feeling of insignificance and worthlessness sank over him. He was lying to Katie and himself again. Using his hand as cushion against the bumps and lurches, he rested his head against the cool glass. There were times when he would persuade himself that everything was all right, that he was doing the right things; he'd run through scenarios in his head where he was happy and content, usually fuzzy memories of the occasional 'great night out', enough times that eventually he believed that he truly was. These stages were usually reached after periods of excessive drinking every day for a week or more. After drinking himself into an appalling depression however, he would refuse to accept or even acknowledge the idea that it was his drinking that was causing the feelings of morbid despair, preferring to blame the world around him; he would tell himself that he was doing what he wanted to do; drinking made him happy; this wasn't depression, he just needed a drink to clear his head, that was all! He noted that he only felt acutely depressed when he was around Katie, or, alternatively the North East of England! What a desperate place, he every right to feel depressed. He got off the bus one stop early, hopping out of the shaking, smoking bus – a peculiar knocking sound coming from the engine – onto the pavement right outside the 'Belmont Arms' pub. By two-thirty, he was no longer insignificant or worthless.

Spencer Chokuwenga, the night watchman, stood scratching his large belly through the well-worn black woolen sweater that was stretched unattractively tight around it like a tea-cozy, bowing the knit pattern into an almost complete circle. He had the bulbous kind of eyes that looked as though they would pop out of their sockets at the slightest increase in his blood pressure. One of his

178

dirty white shirt collars was sticking out of the crew neck of his sweater and his faded black trousers were too short and too tight, making him look as though his mother had dressed him for school. Although only in his forties, he shuffled around, head hanging and shoulders hunched over, like an old man: at night, Jodie would lie awake listening the sound of his feet dragging noisily across the gravel driveway at the side of the house as he did his half-hourly rounds. What would he do if he had to chase someone she often wondered? He was standing in front of the stone fireplace, a beam of sunlight from one of the narrow windows just below the ceiling illuminating his roughly shaved head and the right side of his greasy, bump-riddled face; the bumps casting tiny shadows across his cheek accentuating the coarseness of his skin.

"I don't know Nkosi," he liked to give policemen the title of chief; he believed that they would look more favorably upon him if he ever needed their help. "I had plenty kola, so I was not asleep." He wiped his sleeve across his shiny brow.

"Alice!" Jodie called from the sofa. She turned to the policeman who was standing with his back to the sliding glass doors that lead out onto the verandah. "Would you like some ice water Officer?" The temperature had been rising steadily all morning; the cloudless sky a light, whitewashed blue.

"Yes Madam?" Alice appeared from the hallway. She was dressed plainly in a light green knee-length skirt and a short sleeved, white, low-cut blouse that was bunched at the arms. Her hair was cropped close to her scalp (too close to be attractive Jodie had thought when she'd interviewed Alice for the job), as was the current fashion amongst the young Zimbabwean women. The policeman, recognizing the maid, smiled revealing dazzling white teeth that set against his smooth, near-black skin looked like a bright, crescent moon in a dark night sky; his eyes shone like stars. Alice giggled girlishly and puffed out her chest, enhancing her well-developed bosom.

"No, thank you Alice," he said almost sweetly without acknowledging Jodie's offer. "So," he turned to look at Spencer and continued his 'interrogation' once the maid had disappeared down the dimly lit hallway, his thick local accent becoming more pronounced, "you deed not see anybody anytime daht you was in deh hut." The policeman spoke with a brash, deprecatory tone that Jodie imagined he used only when talking to the black males that were employed by whites as though he were letting them know that he believed them to be of a lower class, less well educated, less virile than he. He was a young man, probably in his late twenties, and Jodie put little faith in his policing abilities. The last two break-ins had been investigated for a short time and abandoned without any kind of reassurances from the police that might have calmed Jodie or Albert. They both knew that the system was corrupt and that none of the items that had been stolen would ever be returned to them, even if any were recovered during the investigation.

"No sah Nkosi, nobody." Spencer scratched the back of his calf with his foot; he had on shiny new-looking army boots. If there was one thing to be said for the man, he took care of his boots. He looked as though he was defying the laws of gravity as he perched, wobbling slightly, on one leg. If he had been a fictional character, Jodie had thought many times, he would most definitely have been Tweedle Dum.

The policeman scribbled something in a small, dog-eared notebook that he had pulled from his crisp, blue shirt pocket earlier. His armpits were ringed with sweat. He mumbled something under his breath and then sucked his teeth noisily.

"It will be very difficult to find the tieves. They have probably sold everyting by now and dehr are not enough policemen to spend deh time on dis kind of crime. Maybe if the police had more people," he paused, "or more money."

Here they were spending Christmas morning with their useless night watchman who smelled as though he hadn't washed in a week, and a corrupt policeman. Jodie turned to look at Albert, polishing his glasses with a white handkerchief and looking slightly scruffy with his shirt tail hanging out of the back of his sleeveless sweater and his shiny, black hair flecked here and there with gray, brushed

181

hurriedly into a crooked parting. He hadn't shaved either, she noted, his (mostly) white beard looking rather unkempt. Albert had discovered the break-in on his way back to the bedroom carrying two mugs of tea on a tray, passing through the living room to pick up the Christmas card he'd bought for Jodie.   Managing to keep his composure as he noticed the open sliding glass door, spilling only a little bit of tea from the mugs onto the tray, he'd inspected the crime scene briefly, noting immediately that all the carefully wrapped presents had been taken from under the small, tastefully decorated Christmas tree as had the Technics record player, the amplifier and speakers, their entire collection of CDs and the portable CD player. It was as he was walking back to the bedroom that he noticed the brick on the floor close to the hallway.

"You were lucky Professor Lewis. Probably Spencer disturbed deh burglars before dey came to your bedroom."

"They must have heard his feet shuffling along the ground," Jodie said suddenly, surprising even herself.

After the policeman had left with his scribbled notes and the brick that he had wrapped in cling-film and stuck into his sweaty armpit, Spencer was given a week's extra pay and a reasonable Christmas bonus and told not to come back. He shuffled out mumbling in Ndebele and scrutinizing the check that Albert had given him as though it was a forgery.

"The Minnards were burgled last night too," Albert said after putting the phone down. Jodie was blowing her nose.

"Pardon? I didn't hear what you said. I think I have a cold coming on." Jodie, staring at the carriage clock on the mantle piece above the fireplace, hadn't moved from the sofa since she'd sat down to wait for the Police to arrive. She sniffled into her handkerchief. How different this living room had felt eleven hours earlier when she and Albert had returned from Midnight Mass at the Anglican Cathedral. A warm and cozy nest, the Christmas tree lights twinkling in some kind of indeterminable pattern, a small number of appealing looking presents propped up to cover the light gray plastic bucket full of rocks (Albert had collected them in preparation for Christmas during a recent weekend sojourn to the ruins of Great Zimbabwe) in which the tree was standing.

"The Minnards dear, they were burgled too. That was Lars on the phone; the Police have just left their place." Albert paused and looked around the living room, aware of the disgruntled look on his face, but unable to erase it. He joined Jodie on the sofa and took hold of her hand. "It could have been worse darling." He had managed to forge a smile.

"I can't wait until your contract is over and we can leave this God forsaken country," she said disparagingly, ignoring his lame attempt to placate her. "Anywhere we go will be better than this, I've had more than enough; even the Bishop warned us all to be careful. You heard what he said last night about the threats he'd received. And all these burglaries? And the carjackings? I'm really unhappy here." She was starting to talk faster; an urgency in her voice that made Albert worry. He had to calm her down quickly, appease her somehow.

"We won't be here for much longer dear; two more semesters and it'll all be over." He stroked the back of her hand delicately, hoping he'd hit the nail on the head and at the same time admiring the softness of her skin.

As he was congratulating himself on his innate deftness for crisis intervention, continuing to caress Jodie's hand, and Jodie beginning to lose herself in the sensation his stroking was giving her, the phone rang making them both jump. Albert tenderly placed Jodie's hand on her lap and got up to answer it.

"Albert Lewis," he said assertively. He felt quite triumphant. "Oh, hello Xavier. Merry Christmas."

Jodie, hearing her son's name, got up and hurried into the study to join in the conversation on the other phone. "Hello Xavier," she said excitedly as soon as she picked up the receiver. The pain of the morning had vanished.

"Hello Mum, Merry Christmas."

As she listened to Xavier speaking, talking about his sudden move back in with Katie, the pending sale of Elizabeth's house in Brandon and the proposed move back to Florida, Jodie began to detect an estranged nuance in his voice, a perfidiousness she had learnt to identify when he

184

had been living at home. A new pain, like a thorn, struck her side and a tear broke suddenly and ran down her cheek. She pulled out her handkerchief from the pocket of her hand-made, ankle-length khaki skirt. Catching the lull in the conversation, she asked Xavier why he and Katie had decided to move to Tampa, of all places.

"A friend of hers from college has been there for about a year and a half and says that house prices are great."

"You're going to buy a house?" The disbelief could not be contained. As the motors whirred, both Albert and Jodie began to complete the puzzle simultaneously.

"Well, Katie thinks it would be better to invest the money in property in America. We both wanted to go back there anyway." The duplicity was becoming more and more apparent and Jodie shook her head sadly. Why was he like this? The room seemed to darken around her, the walls leaning in over her head. She listened to Albert's voice, deep and soothing on the other phone.

"Well, we're glad that you're back together. Oliver must be very happy to have you back. So, when did you move back to Brandon? In your last email, you said that things were going okay at Charlie's."

"Over a week ago. I wrote that email more than two weeks ago. Katie and I talked about Christmas coming up and what would be best for Oliver. I realized that I'd been selfish." Xavier, sensing that a cross-examination had begun tried to fob off his sudden change of heart. "I'd only been thinking about myself. I hadn't been thinking about what Oliver was going through." He spoke with the best submissive, unpretentious tone he could conjure up.

'Or what money you'd be missing out on', Albert mused. This shallowness irked him. He was reminded of Xavier's modeling days: the conceited, egotistic, arrogant young man he'd abruptly turned into; an ugly regression from the heartening self-confidence and pride that bodybuilding had instilled in him a couple of years earlier. Albert heard Jodie sucking her teeth and quickly began speaking.

"Well, I must say that you've certainly made our Christmas Day a lot brighter." He proceeded to recount the vicissitudes of life in Zimbabwe as Xavier listened and "hmm"d in the appropriate places.

'Such was life', he thought, listening as his father rambled on, 'sometimes you're ahead; sometimes you're behind.' He wasn't going to miss this boat, no way. He deserved it: he'd taken care of her plenty of times; worked so hard he'd made himself sick! He found it easy to justify his actions, his change of heart. Albert, Jodie and all of his close friends saw through it all clearly. Katie's eyes however, were looking through rose-colored sunglasses: Xavier did believe in their marriage. He wanted to be with her and Oliver. He did. He truly did. It was just that his love for her was esoteric. It was unique; no one could understand it but her.

And no one did.

Chapter 20: Tampa

Denzil glanced at the clock: '3:57'.

'Aymierda! Como yo voy a terminar esto a tiempo?' He laughed at himself as the thought registered. Xavier had commented during a recent phone call how he could hear the translation delay in Denzil's dialogue. "You've been there too long bro': you're thinking in Spanish."

'There's no way I can possibly get through all this crap before five. I'm not going to put up with this shit anymore,' he told himself (this time in English). He stood up, loosened his tie and then stretching out his massive arms looked around the open plan office with its tiny cubicles: partition walls extending out from his own diminutive cubicle like the hedges of a maze. The walls had not been designed for anyone as tall as him and only came up to his shoulders. He scanned the large room like an army general surveying a battlefield. Here he was coming up on forty, stuck with too big of a workload, his career stagnant, not enough money and an office full of beautiful, wide-hipped Latin women to tempt him every day!

"Focus!" He sat back down at his desk. Sophia and the boys would be waiting for him. He had to get this work done.

Two months earlier, during a fleeting holiday to El Salvador, Xavier had revealed that he was a terrific procrastinator: "I keep saying I'm going to do this and that, but nothing ever ends up getting done. I can't seem to motivate myself. I come up against something that's difficult to do and I give up. I don't know what it is bro'." And the pretty, young dancer that Xavier had taken a fancy to at a strip club who had come back to the house with him on the second night of his holiday had revealed candidly to Denzil a couple of weeks later – having remained in contact with him after Xavier had left in order to keep up to date on the plans to ship her over to America, the idea of which Xavier relished and for a while seriously considered: a gorgeous Latin girl half his age who would cook for him, clean up after him, make love to him twice a day! – the girl had revealed that Xavier was a very sensual and exciting lover; a feeling of pride had risen up inside him then like a coach watching his star player receiving his winning trophy. The two brothers: so similar in so many ways. They had the same two passions: women and booze. Denzil thought back to that magnificent week he'd spent with his brother. Xavier had come to San Salvador primarily to meet his two new nephews and sister-in-law-to-be, but also to get drunk and chase women with his big brother. In England they had always done so well together; a great team. Looking so different (aside from their height and muscularity) had made it extremely easy for the two of them to woo the ladies:

Xavier: "Excuse me, I was just getting a drink for my brother over there," (casually point towards the huge, handsome black guy standing nearby) "and myself. Could I buy you one?"

Lady at bar: "That's not your brother!"

Xavier: "Denzil," (motion for brother to come over) "this young lady doesn't believe that we're brothers!"

(Both present driver's licenses for inspection and the cat was in the bag.)

This ploy had been executed many times with (usually) successful outcomes.

Denzil knew how much his younger brother looked up to him, and had always tried to set a good example. At times though, younger brothers try to emulate the lifestyles that they imagine their older siblings are leading, drawing conclusions from things they see their brother's friends doing – guilty by association – and so some examples may be set through no direct action. But none-the-less, there are good examples and there are *good* examples: the tour of Soho as teenagers was one; athletics was another; marijuana was yet another. Ironically, he found however, that when he had, for a short time lived a saintly life as a 'Born again Christian', Xavier had pulled away from him, finding the indoctrination too extreme and definitely unwelcome. This was no life for an older brother to lead! Luckily for Xavier, that brief period in his life had passed quickly and been forgotten; the hedonistic pleasures of Sodom and Gomorra were far more alluring and rewarding.

The two brothers had spent so much time apart over the last decade that as Xavier was approaching the four of them in the sweaty, jostling arrivals hall of San Salvador International Airport, Denzil had explained forthrightly to Sophia who was carrying Antonio in one arm and holding tightly onto Ben's hand as he wriggled and twisted around like an eel in front of her, that he and his brother had a lot of catching up to do, alone! Xavier, after having been introduced to the family, was whisked off on a splendid tour of San Salvador's many strip clubs and brothels by Denzil and Mike, an English friend (who owned a car). A week later, unable to walk properly and carrying the heart of a young Salvadorian girl, having promised to send her some shoes, Xavier had returned to the mess he'd left behind in Tampa.

Pushing against his desk, Denzil tilted himself back in his wheeled chair against the flimsy wall behind him. He spent a few moments motivating himself and was just about to start working through the stack of cases in his in-box when someone called his name from another cubicle somewhere in the middle of the battlefield. "Denzil! Telephono!"

He rocked forward unsteadily before ungracefully righting the chair back onto the clear plastic matting that lined the floors of every cubicle. Hesitantly, he reached for the phone. "Denzil Lewis," he said in his standard deep, authoritative phone voice.

"Buenos dios. Kay pasa ninyo?"

"Eh!" Denzil laughed out loud at Xavier's comic Spanish, relieved that it wasn't a business call that would undoubtedly have given him a headache. "Hello Bro'! It's good to hear from you. How are you?"

Xavier had recently begun to wonder why it was that his brother always spoke in perfect Queen's English after so many years away from England. He had decided that it must be because Denzil now very rarely spoke English and so when he did it, was recalled, untainted by subtle alterations that come from constantly having to repeat one's self – "Whadya say?" – from the depths of his speech memory. Over the years in America, Xavier's once posh-sounding Queen's (Colonial) English, which at school had caused him numerous untold beatings and head-flushings in urinals by the narrow-minded bullies (usually from Brandon or the adjoining town of Meadowfield), had developed a twang that gave his voice a slight Australian character that he abhorred. He had resolutely refused to lower himself to say 'warder' for 'warter' or 'tomaydo' for 'tomarto' or 'skedule' for

191

'sheduel' though, much to the delight of young American women, who on the whole found his accent adorable, and he was trying to make sure that Oliver grew up speaking English, not American.

"I'm okay. I wanted to talk to you." There was a short pause. "Katie's talking about getting a divorce. She says that she's had enough." If there was any sadness in Xavier's voice, Denzil couldn't detect it.

"Are you going to go through with it?" He recalled how two years earlier he had been the one making this same phone call.

"She told me that I have to. A friend of hers knows a mediator who's going to draw up the papers. She's going to get everything."

"I thought that you were going to leave her anyway?" Denzil left it as a rhetorical question and continued. "Have you moved out?"

"Yeah, I've been staying with a friend." Xavier's voice suddenly brightened making Denzil realize that hadn't read his brother's tone very well. "I met this girl at an Irish pub last week. Ana, a beautiful little Sicilian thing. She's a PHD student at USF here in Tampa." Denzil heard his brother chuckle. "Bro', I tell you, she's gorgeous!"

"What is she studying?"

"Anthropology."

"Anthropology. Wow! She must be pretty intelligent, so what's she doing with you? Well, I guess if she's anything like Jane Goodall then she'll certainly enjoy your company from a research standpoint." Denzil laughed loud and heartily at his own joke before abruptly shutting up, remembering that he was at work. "Why don't you bring her here. I'll make sure that Camille doesn't find out you're in the country. Well, we won't be going to any of the clubs anyway if Annie comes with you."

"Ana," Xavier corrected his brother, "I'd love to come back and bring Ana so you can meet her."

Denzil could tell that Xavier was smitten once again. He had an old cassette tape somewhere of a few songs by the band that Xavier had been in with Charlie. He smiled as one verse of the song entitled, *I'm with Stupid ('cos Stupid buys all the drinks)*, written by the band's lead singer in celebration of Xavier's caprice and generosity played in his mind:

"Love is the best, I've been saving till last.

I've this friend, he's called Xavier, falls in love at first glance.

I've always thought that was a gift until now,

but imagine the cost when Christmas comes round."

"So, are you going to move in with this new girl?" Denzil was still smiling at the image of Xavier laden with a towering stack of Christmas presents trying to make sure each of his girlfriends received the correct one.

"I don't think so, she knows I'm still married. And I need some time to enjoy my freedom." Xavier tone was darkening rapidly. "I've been trapped for too long."

"I know exactly what you mean. Take care of your heart bro', don't let this girl hurt you."

"I won't. I'll keep things in perspective. She's lovely, but I'll make sure I don't fall in too deep." Xavier cleared his throat and tried to convince himself that he believed what he had just said.

"So when will the divorce go though?"

"I'm not sure, Katie has only just started talking about this. We'll see what happens."

'So much time has passed; so much pain and resentment. A new life started with boundless ambition and hope and yet, here I am again, older and more mature but still not the right man for you Katie. I'm not happy this way.'

Xavier put down the pen and looked out over the pool at the illuminated living rooms of the houses across the lake. 'This is it. This will be the end of us,' he thought. Xavier had always found it more comfortable to communicate his inner feelings through writing. He was much more likely to express himself openly if he had pen and paper in front of him rather than prying, analyzing eyes and probing questions. A soft breeze tried to lift one corner of the paper and Xavier put his hand on the sheet of white paper to keep it from blowing off the glass table. The lanai was his favorite part of the two-story house. He was going to miss it. Sometimes he found peace out here at night after Katie and Oliver had gone off to sleep. He could drink and smoke to his heart's content, watching the lights across the lake, imagining what kinds of lives were being lived in those houses; whether those people were happy or going through the same shit that he was. His time at the house was sporadic. He came and went as he pleased, Katie allowing this after a tremendous argument during which Xavier had smacked a soup spoon off his forehead, drawing blood, and had told her that she couldn't keep him from seeing his son. Another time she tried to persuade him make his mind up to stay or go, he had punched a hole in a wall in the hallway by the laundry room, covering it the next day with a framed photograph of Katie and Oliver taken during the holiday in Tenerife. Since the first time he hadn't come home, Katie had desperately fought the feeling of resignation, the grave idea that the marriage was over and that he was only there because of Oliver and the pool. She had eventually stopped fighting.

"Don't do this Katie." The words were meant for the paper. He chewed the inside of his lips, hoping she hadn't heard him.

The house was dark and silent; Katie was massaging her shins and raised her head when she heard him speak, his voice no louder than a breath. An airplane passed low over the house, its jets thundering, on its approach to Tampa International Airport only four miles south. The flashing lights were reflected in the pool, its surface as smooth as glass. Katie waited for the roar of its engines to fade.

"This is the only way. There's too much dirty water under the bridge. Once the divorce has gone through, then we'll

see. If you want to get back together, you can try then."
She looked out into the darkness, her breathing soft and
shallow. "I need to do this for me."

Xavier squinted his eyes, the deep furrows in his forehead
felt like tight bands tied around his head. Once again, he
had lost all the passion for this life; maybe the next one
would be better.

"But where would we go? There aren't any other
options: it's not as though there are Universities lining up
to hire me. I know I promised that we'd move, but we
simply can't." Albert uncrossed his legs and stood up,
stretching his back out. He went into the study, returning a
minute later with a brown paper folder.

"Yes, I know that you've done all you can dear," Jodie said
before Albert could start with his review of institutions he
had applied to. She was shaking her head, a fragile smile
forming that looked as though it was being forced, but
sincerity and compassion conspicuous in her gray-blue
eyes. "I knew that it would be more difficult than we
thought it would."

It amazed Albert that at such precious times, Jodie could
always maintain her composure. He hadn't noticed it much
before the move from Northern Cyprus, but her ability to
remain calm under stress had improved remarkably over
the last few years.

"Let's have some tea. Why don't you put the kettle on?"

He obeyed with alacrity. In the kitchen, as he filled the kettle at the sink, he noticed a dim, orange glow in the darkness that looked at first glance like the beginning of a vibrant sunrise, typical in the thin air of Bulawayo, but remembering the direction the window faced, Albert quickly realized that true east was a little further to the left; and anyway, the sun had set not more than three hours earlier. At first he couldn't determine at what distance it was from the house, but as the topography mapped out from his memory, he calculated that it must have been coming from one of the farms on the way to the Eastern Highlands. "Not again!" he said to himself and decided against mentioning it. 'Another three years' bounced around his head as he prepared a pot of tea. At this moment, more than ever, he wished he had Jodie's conviction and resilience; wished he could feel the same hope; share her bright optimism; believe in himself as she believed in him.

There is in some weak people who feel their own weakness and resent it, a certain process, which, operating suddenly and without conscious direction, releases them from final humiliation. Xavier, who up until recently had been viewing his lifestyle as grand, something to be envied, now abruptly lost his temper.

"Fucking bastard!" He was too angry to respond to Charlie's email and shut the computer down at the 'off' button. "Fuck you too!"

For a while he had been a legend amongst his friends in Durham, the first one to break away from the stagnancy of life in the North East of England, but as time passed, as the news he'd bring back with him on periodic holidays or share in letters and phone calls began to show no discernable progression in his emotional development or in his career, Xavier soon became somewhat of an object of ridicule. He had always been a clown, but he had become a fool in the eyes of his close friends. The first few homecomings had been celebrations; his friends all glad to see him, a veritable prodigal son, honored that he had taken time out of his fabulous life in America to come back to see them; amazed at his opulence as he distributed packets of cigarettes that he and Katie brought over with them as though they grew on trees in America; they would make appointments to meet up with him, call other friends to arrange a 'big night out'; listen with profound interest when he spoke of the huge cars, cheap petrol, beautiful beaches, the steamy climate, the thick, gray sheets of rain that would fall on one side of the street and not the other, the American girls who loved a man with an English accent – these astounding stories had been corroborated a few times by the odd friend who'd managed to make it over to visit Katie and Xavier. (Once during a visit from two of his friends to Burlingame, Xavier had found himself, the day they arrived, having to separate the two men who, behaving like children who had to share a toy,

198

had been squabbling noisily over who was going to be the first to drive the fantastic Cadillac.) For a few years he had enjoyed the two weeks of being put up on a pedestal; enjoyed seeing Katie squirm, unable to quell the tide of attention that he was being given – Katie's old school friends showed much less interest in her life away from the North East of England, perhaps feeling more jealousy than envy. But eventually, as with all good things, the gig was over. One by one, the friends began losing interest in the life of the rapacious fool; they bought houses, got better jobs, enjoyed their marriages and children, settled happily into adult life. Xavier's holidays and letters and phone calls became fewer and farther between until the internet became his sole means of communication with his 'old friends' – usually used as a slate for his moaning and whining. The final cord was severed when Xavier received the unexpected and shocking reply to an emotionally charged email that he'd sent to Charlie describing yet another low point in his woebegone life.

'Sort your fucking life out Xav! You're a father now, stop living as though you're still a kid. If you're planning on coming back here you're not welcome in our house. You can't keep running away from your responsibilities. Get yourself some fucking help!' Charlie wasn't holding back when he'd written to Xavier this time and Xavier didn't appreciate his 'old friend's' bluntness; his honesty. At least, not for a while.

Chapter 21: Introspection

Selfishness was a character trait that Albert believed wholeheartedly he didn't possess. As did Xavier and Denzil. The three Lewis men saw themselves as generous, giving, empathetic, sympathetic, non-competitive people. The truth was that they were in fact overly non-competitive, too unassertive and submissive for their own good. They were generous, there was certainly no doubt about that. The three men had always felt happier helping the less fortunate in whatever way they could; felt more at ease around people who had very little. Achievements, they believed, were not measured by how many possessions one had accumulated, how much money one had stashed away in a bank somewhere, but rather, how many people one had helped in one way or another. Although as adults Denzil and Xavier would both end up living very simple lives with simple needs, as boys – as most children do as they grow older – they had always talked of buying this car and that one, owning a large, fancy house, dreamed of living in the lap of luxury, being waited on hand and foot, spending their days at the beach or relaxing by a pool or reading and writing, composing music, playing in bands, owning their own companies. This vision of utopia was evoked by their memories of their life in Ghana; a biased, contorted view clouded mainly by time. Albert and Jodie also looked back with fond memories of their many years in that beautiful country. Once, sometime before the move to Zimbabwe, sitting outside a café overlooking the harbor in Kyrenia, waiting for Jodie who was shopping for a dress or a pair of shoes, Albert had noticed two boys rolling hoops along the waterfront using sticks and he was reminded of a boy he had played the same game with at school in Croydon. Dwelling on this long-forgotten joyful memory of a childhood friend, it had struck Albert as odd that one either only has pleasant memories of a situation, person or place or distressing ones; very rarely both. For the most part, life in Ghana had been wonderful for the whole family – more of a paradise for the boys than most children could ever claim to have experienced – but occasionally, as a result of some abstract trigger, an aroma perhaps, or a piece of music, the clouds would be thinned momentarily allowing a glimpse of the parts that had been carefully shrouded, painstakingly forgotten for one reason or another.

Albert listened, horrified at the sound coming from across the back garden, as Baby Kofi screamed: the screams of a boy being beaten hard; harder than he had ever hit Xavier or Denzil. There was raging anger, wild fury in this beating. From across the living room, illuminated by two wall lights on either side of the doors that led out to the veranda and a tall hand carved wooden lamp with a cream pyramidal shade that stood in the corner behind the grand piano, Xavier's grin could be seen: justice was being done. He was sitting on the floor quietly playing with his collection of Matchbox cars. The screaming stopped abruptly and the house was eerily quiet apart from the incessant percussive chirping of crickets that seemed to be coming from all around. As the next song on the Simon and Garfunkel record began – *Bridge over troubled water*, he thought – the screaming started again. Albert got up and closed the two windows behind him. The light was fading into the gray of evening. The ceiling fan turned lazily, humming, gently stirring the warm, humid air.

Albert tried to recall what time of year it had been: late summer, the end of the wet season maybe. The memory disturbed him, but he was going to allow it to unfold. He took a sip of wine and gazed out across the valley, the lush green forest glowing luminescently in the fading light, beneath flamingo-pink and mango-orange clouds. There were lights coming on below the cottage and to the left – the village of Chimanimani. Albert felt as though he and Jodie were in a different world, far removed from the torments of Bulawayo, the burglaries and carjackings; safe from harm. He put the glass down and uncrossed his legs, extending them out and as he felt the muscles stretching,

202

let out a long, quiet, satisfied moan. His body ached more than ever these days. His leather sandals were dusty from the long walk that he and Jodie had gone on that afternoon from the cottage down the brush-covered side of the hillside, following a narrow, winding path to the base of the waterfall. Bridal Veil, a high fall, fell like fine lace over black-ridged rock into a deep, dark pool. Refilling the water bottle and dipping his hands into the pool and wiping the back of his neck, Albert had found the water to be refreshingly chilly and delicious, unspoiled by human intervention, having traveled down from the springs high up in the Eastern Highlands where they were staying.

Albert let his memory wander back to that odd episode in Nhyaesu…

Xavier had come to him as he was working in the study – the square room with windows on all four sides, above the doorless storage space where the children would scamper about singing loudly as he worked above them – sometime after lunch. It was a Saturday afternoon. Xavier had complained that his Matchbox ambulance was missing. Later, throughout dinner, he had whined and sobbed like a baby about how the toy had been in the bedroom that morning with all of his other Matchbox cars but now it was gone. Albert and Jodie had tried to placate him, promising to replace the ambulance on Monday when the shops would be open. Denzil had even offered to give him one of his own cars. But nothing had consoled poor Xavier and he had gone to bed crying softly, just loud enough for everyone to hear. The following afternoon, on the way back from the University swimming pool, they had stopped at the shantytown to buy some kenkey (fermented corn flour rolled in a banana leaf which is boiled until tender), smoked fish and pepper sauce to have with supper. It had been just as they were about to get back into the car that Xavier had spotted something and started shouting, "Daddy! Daddy!" Everyone turned to see what the boy was creating such a fuss about. A couple of vendors down from the kenkey seller, on a low wooden table, laid out with some other children's toys, some a little worse for wear, was a small white Matchbox ambulance. It was Xavier's. Kofi had been sent for to translate the Twi for them and it was soon determined that Baby Kofi had exchanged the toy the day before for some food; the young Ashanti girl manning the table couldn't recall what food her mother had given to him in exchange for the toy. No attempts to calm Xavier had worked, and even with his toy back in his possession and repeated assurances from Kofi that Baby Kofi would be punished, he remained livid, upset that Baby Kofi had had the audacity to steal one of his toys from his bedroom. Baby Kofi had been out doing an errand for his father and hadn't returned home until a couple of hours later. And now he was being severely punished.

Albert asked Xavier why he was smiling. Xavier said he didn't like anyone else playing with his toys. Baby Kofi shouldn't have been playing with *his* toys. To Albert, it

204

seemed as if Xavier had externalized himself from the retribution that Kofi was administering to his son, refusing to let himself feel that he was in any way responsible for the screams that seemed to linger in the warm, evening air: the boy had done something wrong and deserved to be punished.

"Will you be able to make it to Tessa's Pool tomorrow?" Jodie was standing in the doorway that led inside the cottage, holding her empty wineglass, smiling at this scene: her aging husband (his beard now almost entirely white, but his hair still holding on steadfastly to its dark color), lost in memories, rubbing his thighs, clad in safari-style shorts, his legs stretched out resting on his dusty heels.

"Oh hello dear. I was just day dreaming." He motioned with his head for her to join him on the uncushioned wicker sofa. "More wine?"

Jodie sat down next to him and offered her glass up as Albert poured out some more of the South African Shiraz. She sat back and began admiring the view and enjoying the tranquility, the stillness. All around were sounds of wildlife. The strange noises didn't make you feel uneasy or afraid, as if you were a foreigner, separated from this untamed world and yet intruding at the same time, and especially when combined with the homely feel of the Frog and Fern Cottages, the way they had been carefully designed to blend into the landscape, you felt more as though you were an intrinsic part of it all, at one with nature. After a minute or two, she broke the repose. "What were you thinking about?"

"Xavier." There was a short pause. "When he was a boy." A sparse frown sat on his forehead for a moment; Jodie caught it as it was leaving. For a moment she could not discern what it was, until she saw the distance in his eyes.

"He still is, in some ways." Jodie was being drawn in to the melancholy. "I'm worried about him." As she formulated her thoughts, she found it funny that she did feel a concern for Xavier's well being. He was a grown man, living in one of the richest countries in the world, in a stable economy with opportunities around every corner, whereas she and Albert were scraping by in a country that had one of the worst economies in the world, ruled by a white-hating dictator, victims of burglaries and carjackings that the Police could not (or rather cared not to) deal with, having to queue for hours to buy petrol, having to travel across the border to South Africa or Botswana to buy groceries. And she was worried about Xavier?

On Monday morning, after a light breakfast of toast and orange marmalade, two cups of Nescafé and a freshly picked star fruit each (in addition to the beautiful purple and pink bougainvillea, the dainty gladiolus, the bushy hibiscus with their giant red flowers, and numerous other tropical flowering plants and bushes, the grounds around the Frog and Fern Cottages were planted with a wonderful assortment of fruit trees – paw paw, sour sop, star fruit, mango, avocado – that, during the hot summer months, October to March, would be over-laden with fruit; fruit that the guests were encouraged to help themselves to), after breakfast, Albert and Jodie packed up and headed back to Bulawayo. The road down to the plains from Chimanimani was nothing more than a dusty, narrow farm track; unpaved and poorly maintained. Outside of the major towns, the infrastructure had crumbled disastrously over the last year or so as the farm invasions continued and the white farmers were either murdered or thrown out of the country. The war veterans who now inhabited the vast areas of farmland had neither the knowledge nor the means (and certainly didn't have the inclination) to tend to the countryside surrounding them: Mugabe would take care of them. Mugabe was going to provide food for the heroes. They merely consumed what produce there was left growing in the fields or had been stored in the massive barns that the white farmers, sensing trouble, had built and begun filling as soon as President Mugabe had won the last election, a short time afterwards, ordering the land invasions. As the aging Volkswagen bumped its way along, Jodie mentally prepared herself for the return home. As hard as she tried to vanquish the fears that were crawling all about her like snakes, attempted to conjure up happy childhood memories (no mean feat as they were few and far between), she could feel her heart rate increasing and an itchiness, like prickly heat, germinating under her skin even with one arm out of the window, her hand dreamily riding the cool wind – something she imagined she might have done as a child. Albert hardly spoke during the three-hour drive, the cool breeze from the open window wafting his hair. 'Everything will be alright, everything will be alright', he repeated to himself over and over.

Samuel Mpofu lay in the hospital bed, his head swathed in bandages, his life discernable only by the intermittent beeping of the heart monitor and the slight rising and falling of his stomach. 'Maybe that's the machine doing that,' Albert contemplated. There were wires and tubes coming from numerous places on his body connected to various machines and drips. Albert was glad that he hadn't brought Jodie with him; she was safe at the neighbor's house. Albert turned to see Alice entering the room, smiling.

"Hello Sir, how was deh weekend?" Alice, as always, seemed to be lost in her own little world.

Albert, skipping the pleasantries, spoke sternly.

"What happened Alice? Where are the Police?"

"I don't know Sir. Maybe dey was at deh house after Mr. Howard called dem. I came here in deh car with Mr. Howard and Samuel. Deh doctor ask me what I had seen. I'm sorry Sir, but I did not hear anyting las night."

Albert chewed the inside of his lower lip, breathing heavily through his nose. A short, bald white man, in his fifties perhaps, with thin wire framed rectangular glasses perched

208

on the end of his shiny, stubby nose, dressed in a green doctor's gown entered the room carrying a clipboard under his arm. He had his prerequisite stethoscope around his neck and held himself purposefully with an air of egotistic dignity. Albert cleared his throat to introduce himself, but before he managed to get a word out, the man spoke, reaching his hand forward as he approached, his teeth flashing.

"Hello, I'm Doctor Martin. You must be Professor Lewis." The man's thick cockney accent threw Albert, leaving him speechless for a moment.

"Yes. Hello Doctor. Nice to meet you." Albert shook the doctor's hand firmly.

"Newcastle, I understand."

"I beg your pardon?"

"Newcastle," the doctor repeated, louder this time as though speaking to a child.

"Oh, yes. Well, for a few years anyway. I taught at the University."

"Yes, yes. I know." He left this statement hanging, Albert's mind buzzing as he contemplated how this man could know he had been at Newcastle University, and walked over to the bed.

"So, bad thing, this beating. Iron bar. He's lucky to be alive. Your neighbor got him here just in time."

Albert tried to interject, but the man spoke as though reading a monologue and could not be interrupted until he had finished reading his part. He had his clipboard in his hands and was studying it intently. There was a smell that Albert couldn't identify; it wasn't the typical hospital smell, but more like some kind of vegetable. It faded as surreptitiously as it had risen.

"It seems that the neighbor's watchman heard the disturbance and woke everyone up with his shouting. From what I've gathered…"

As he spoke, Albert wondered whether perhaps he'd been a policeman in London before becoming a doctor.

"…Alice," he nodded towards her, "came here with Samuel in the neighbor's car. I've questioned her briefly. Your neighbor is responsible for saving his life." He paused for a second, taking a deep breath as he squinted his beady brown eyes through his glasses at the beeping monitor on the other side of the bed and then continued. "He's still unconscious; lost a lotta blood. He won't be talking to you any time soon. There could well be damage to the brain." The doctor stopped speaking abruptly.

Albert waited to see if there was any more coming. Doctor Martin looked up from his clipboard inquisitively as though puzzled as to why Albert wasn't speaking.

"I, er, we have to get home to make sure everything's okay. We have a cat." As soon as the words had come out, Albert felt embarrassed by them.

"Well, I'll call you if there're any changes in his condition. He nodded once again towards Alice. "Your maid gave me your phone number. Nice to meet you Professor Lewis." The doctor extended his hand once more and put on a face full of empathy that Albert knew was as fake as the perfectly straight white teeth in the man's mouth.

"Thank you Doctor." Albert left, still nonplussed as to how the doctor could know of his time at Newcastle University with Alice following silently.

Back at the house, Albert and Alice checked around for any damage. Whoever had beaten Samuel had been disturbed before managing to break into the house. The iron bar that had been used by the burglars lay on the stoep, dried blood all over it and on the paving stones where Samuel had fallen. After instructing Alice to try and clean up the blood – using rubber gloves – from the stoep, Albert put on a pair of thick gardening gloves that were lying along with a trowel in Jodie's trug that was close by and picked up the iron bar at a section that had no blood on it (with the Aids epidemic rampant throughout the countries of Southern Africa, one couldn't be too careful) and carried it to the back of the house where he washed it off with the hose and locked it away in the sturdy, brick tool shed. After having made sure that everything in the house was present and correct, he collected Jodie from the Howard's.

Xavier opened the letter from Zimbabwe being careful not to tear the $5400 stamp – with the country's inflation rate at somewhere around four hundred percent, the Zimbabwe Dollar was practically worthless and still, even at the equivalent of $21(US), the letter had taken almost a month to travel to Florida – the attractive stamp depicting a jar of herbs (*Medicinal Herb: Cleome Nyevhe, Ulede*, was the title), and with a fresh beer sat down at the patio table outside the sliding glass doors of the kitchen to read the latest news from Zimbabwe. He lit a cigarette before beginning; 'what bad news this time?' (The emails from his father always brushed over the bad news, giving him weather reports and narratives of idyllic weekend sojourns. The letters on the other hand, usually written by his mother, gave fairly in-depth reports of the mess that the country was in and the hardships they were enduring. This one certainly was no exception.)

'…We eventually arrived back in Bulawayo on Monday afternoon to find that there had been an attempted break-in the previous night at about 3.30am. The watchman, Samuel Mpofu had been badly beaten about the head with an iron bar, collapsing unconscious. The watchman next door heard the disturbance and woke Mr. Howard, his employer. He came around immediately and took him to the hospital. Samuel would have undoubtedly died from his injuries and loss of blood if he hadn't been taken to hospital so promptly. Even though the attempted murder was reported to the police, they haven't been near the place. Albert moved the iron bar into the tool shed, and it's just as well he did, because there was another attempted break-in a few days later (before we'd managed to find a new watchman).

212

The burglars forced the kitchen door open, but fortunately were unable to open the metal security grill. They used two mops to try unsuccessfully to pull things from the veranda. Meanwhile, we have had a lot of welcome rain, and finally all the bloodstains have been washed away. The police have been absolutely useless, and in all our burglaries have made no attempt to apprehend the criminals nor to recover the stolen goods. What do these brave chaps do?'

Xavier's cigarette had burnt down leaving a fragile sweep of ash. He flicked it into the grass and lit another; little pieces of ash danced around him gaily on the soft breeze. The letter went on to describe the atrocities that the police, no better than armed thugs, were inflicting on people who spoke out against Mugabe, in particular the Roman Catholic Archbishop, Pius Ncube, and how a week or so earlier, a friend of a friend, an elderly lady who taught music at a local school, was brutally murdered as she walked home from school. The letter ended with a brief description of one of Albert's student's wedding that they had attended. Xavier had finished three beers in the time it took him to read the letter from his mother. He went inside, letting the cool air embrace him for a minute, and opened another beer.

'They need to get the fuck out!' he said to himself. Back outside, he picked the letter up again and stared at the typewriter print on the paper. He smiled as he looked over his mother's typing and at the frequent use of whiteout. He lit another cigarette and gazed up at the fluffy clouds drifting by in the crystal blue sky overhead.

Two days later, after many hours of soul-searching without beer as a guide, Xavier finally put pen to paper. He was ready to expose his weaknesses, to explain to his parents exactly how he felt before it was too late. This was it. Gritting his teeth determinedly, he began…

'Dear Mum and Dad,
I've been meaning to write to you for ages, but have never felt ready to let my feelings out. But, I'm going to in this letter.
There is an emptiness inside me, a deep, soul-blinding void that I have been trying to fill for many, many years. I have mutated this emptiness into a life debilitating sadness, allowing this sadness to progress so far that I have required therapy and medication for the treatment of depression. I also tried to find happiness by surrounding myself with adoring friends (fans) hoping that an over-inflated ego would help reduce the pain. Alcohol also seemed to keep it at bay. However, nothing so far has worked. The pain is still there. The emptiness just as expansive. Everything I've tried to do to ease my daily existence has done nothing except cloud my mind and caused me to hurt those who've tried to love me. We all have individual needs. I have come to realize that I do have simple needs: peace; tranquility; happiness; oneness; good friends. Chuang Po-Tuang

214

breaks it down in his book, *Inner Teachings of Taoism*: True Intent; True Sense; Spiritual Essence. These are the three central principles that one must fathom before complete enlightenment can be attained. Introspection is the first step that I've taken. At thirty-five years old, I was well overdue for some good old soul-searching. My first session left me feeling downright disgusted with myself, the 'qualities' I found: a blatant disregard for the feelings of others; a friendship destroying ego; a belief that I was invincible; an ugly lack of respect – not only for those who loved me, but also for my own self.

I had for many years lived my life as though I was the center of the Universe. Bodybuilding (for which I developed a great passion for) and modeling gave me an inner strength as great as I had as a child growing up in Ghana. I had lost that childhood 'power' when we moved to England. There, I quickly lost most of my faith in myself, in you, in people, in life. I withdrew into a dark corner, finding a glimmer of light in music – a passion you both instilled in me from a very early age. For that, I thank you.

The transition from Ghana to England was traumatic for me. I found life much more complicated, people much less friendly. I yearned for my home, my utopian existence. I went through a period of growing resentment towards you, my parents, for taking me away from all that we had had in Ghana. The result of this growing resentment was rebellion. I decided that I would go against everything that

215

you wanted for me. My school work suffered. My morals and ethics dissipated (I tried to kill a boy who bullied me at school!) I fought and fought, adamant that I was going to ignore all your attempts to teach me, to guide me down the path of life you had mapped out for me. You assumed that I would find a purpose that would keep me straight and focused. What you didn't account for was the pain that I've been feeling for over fifteen years since we left Ghana. It is a pain that draws me down, makes me search for something, something just out of my reach. There is an answer out there for me. There has to be a life that is easier to endure than this present one. There has to be!

I have striven for years to control the loss of conscious thought that deprived me of the ability to form goals, develop ambitions. So far, I'm about as far down as I can cope with at the moment; not as low as I have been at times: when I was living in Sheffield; in San Francisco and Fort Lauderdale; at times I wished that I would die. All I wanted was a little bit of love to take the pain away – love in my own heart, not love from another (that I've had but never truly appreciated).

I find myself comparing my parenting abilities to yours in an attempt to put everything into perspective. I've tried to blame this and that on you both. I go around in circles hoping that I'll discover the reasons that I do some things and don't do others.

I can't go on blaming you for everything. I love you both, Xavier.'

Xavier let out a deep sigh, as though he'd been holding his breath the entire time that he'd been writing. Without proofing the letter, he folded it and slid it into the envelope that he had brought outside in readiness. This was a major step for him. A huge weight had been lifted from his shoulders and he felt elated that he'd managed to get all that emotion, that hurt, which had been bottled up for so many years, out onto paper. But, as with most of Xavier's 'major accomplishments', the euphoria of success didn't last long. The fractures of doubt quickly began to form in his mind. Nothing that he ever did was right; nothing was ever good enough. What was he trying to do? How would his parents react when they read that he blamed them for his sadness, his weakness?

'Shit! Fucking shit! You useless fucker!' Xavier ripped up the letter, set the pieces of paper alight with his Zippo, stormed inside the house and rolled another joint.

Chapter 22: Realization

'I don't want to ever see you or hear from you again. You have a problem Xavier and need help. Real, tangible help. What you have done is beyond my comprehension. You are a horrid, selfish man. You have hurt me but more importantly, you have hurt Oliver. Don't try to contact me. Just get yourself some help. Soon. Oh, and BTW, you can buy your shit back at Goodwill!'

The words, read with a lucid mind, had more of an impact. When he had first read the email that Debbie had sent to him three months earlier, her emotionally charged words had bounced off him like water off a duck's back. He turned to look outside. The two dogs were sitting up against the sliding glass doors in the shade of the eaves, staring at him with their best pathetic look, their eyebrows rising to meet in the center of their foreheads, their tongues hanging, salivating. The large garden behind them was overgrown with grass and weeds, empty beer bottles lay here and there, a gray tee shirt was trampled into the dirt, there were cigarette butts and roaches everywhere. There were so many of them that to a visitor they might, at first glance, have appeared to be little white blossoms. This house, with its unkempt garden in Land O Lakes, ten miles north of Tampa, was dirty. The entire house smelt of dogs and their urine. The uncarpeted concrete floor was filthy and would turn the soles of your feet black. Xavier continued to live here because his roommate Josh, who owned the house, charged him very little rent and there was always beer in the fridge. He sent the email back to the 'Girlfriends' folder he had created after the divorce and logged out of his Yahoo! account. 'What an asshole! She was perfect for you; they've all been perfect for you.' The insides of his cheeks were sore from his chewing. A wave of pressure washed over his chest as he got up and walked down the dark hallway to his bedroom. He lay on the bed, his breathing labored, the pressure on his chest increasing, his ribs contracting painfully, and stared at the textured ceiling, light from the window at the head of the bed casting shadows off the tiny peaks, creating patterns that seemed to form and dissipate as he watched, constantly changing and moving as though the ceiling was the surface of some enchanted, bubbling, white liquid. All around was cool, silent air. He felt a sudden, darting pain in his left side that made him flinch. 'Maybe this was a heart attack. If only it could be this easy. If only!' He imagined himself gasping for air, panicking, flailing, like a fish out of water, unable to comprehend what was happening, what was taking its life away. The pressure on his chest was gone as swiftly as it had come; the patterns on the ceiling constantly changing as he lay watching, still, silent. Outside, it was oddly quiet. The ceiling was now the surface of a mysterious new planet waiting to be explored – a place where no-one knew who he was; a world in which all the mistakes he had made had been erased; a world where he would feel no pain whenever he looked back on his life; a place where he was innocent and free and happy.

A new life, a new history (keeping the years spent in Ghana of course!), a past that wasn't littered with the crap that he had left along the way in this one: he'd be able to look at his reflection in the mirror without a feeling of disgust overwhelming him; he would no longer be afraid to look into his own eyes, and when he did, in place of failure, weakness and anger, he would see honesty, integrity, inner strength, pride, love; he'd recall times gone by when he had been loved and had treasured the love that had been offered to him and hadn't abused it, discarded it; he'd be empathetic and capable enough to see those around him who didn't understand the way he lived, personifying their suspicions through acts of bullying, not as ignorant and deserving to die but rather, merely needy recipients of his patience and understanding. That was all he wanted.

At thirteen, Ian Cummings was a hulking boy. His spine curved as it neared his neck, his broad shoulders drooped forward over his chest, his thick arms hung loosely, swinging like elephant trunks, his large head, topped with a shaggy mop of black hair sat firmly on his short neck, his voice had already broken completely and he had a dark – albeit feathery – moustache. He lived in Brandon and his nickname was 'The Hunchback'. On Tuesdays and Thursdays, he sat next to Xavier during the double French period before lunch and again next to him in Geography after lunch. It wasn't that Ian thought Xavier was a nice person or that he was his friend. Or that he even liked anything at all about Xavier. Anything that is, except for the fact that he could pick on the much weaker, insecure Xavier and get away with it. Xavier's reputation as being a feeble, meek boy who would take a beating or head-flushing in a urinal or toilet without squealing was fairly well known throughout Johnston Comprehensive School in Durham. Ian had, for some time, been one of Xavier's least favorite people on Earth, and here he was, sitting next to him four times a week. Xavier's puny left upper arm was almost constantly bruised from the punches that Ian would unleash whenever he had the opportunity, when the teacher was facing the blackboard or sitting engrossed in a textbook. Xavier had learnt that it was better to keep quiet about these routine beatings, as the one time he had raised his arm and asked Mrs. White if there was any way his desk could be moved away from Ian's, later that day, during break period, aside from the usual beating, The Hunchback and a few of his friends had let Xavier know, in no uncertain terms, that any more clever moves like that would be dealt with severely. Xavier never again attempted any kind of clandestine operation to release himself from the grip of The Hunchback. Indeed, he believed that there was nothing that could be done; there was no escape. (A year later, Xavier was to take up bodybuilding with an intense passion; a passion fueled by images of one day standing face to face with The Hunchback and making him apologize for the months of torture he had put Xavier through, however, at the time, the idea of standing up to The Hunchback and making him apologize was the furthest thing from Xavier's mind.) All he could do now was to sit back and take the beatings silently, bravely; each Tuesday and Thursday going to school compliantly, accepting that a sore arm was inevitable. That was until The Hunchback decided that he needed to increase his caloric intake and that Xavier was to aid him in this quest.

At lunch time, Xavier, living within a mile of the school, walked home every day, escaping the great anguish that spending an entire lunch hour in the vicinity of The Hunchback would have caused – the attacks weren't restricted to Tuesdays and Thursdays: there were plenty of opportune moments during break times in the morning and the afternoon and PE for him to have his fun. At home though, Xavier was safe from harm; his private troubles were a million miles away. Then, one Tuesday during French, The Hunchback told Xavier that he wanted him to make a peanut butter and strawberry jam sandwich while he was at home during lunch that Ian was going to eat just before Geography started. In his usual abject manner, Xavier obeyed. A couple of weeks later, his appetite increasing as a result of a growth spurt (like he needed it!), The Hunchback demanded that two sandwiches be made for him. The sandwiches became The Hunchback's twice-weekly standing order.

Xavier had always been a studious boy with an innate desire to learn. He wasn't particularly fond of sciences preferring languages and the arts, but he gradually began to appreciate the mysteries of Physics and Chemistry: all those theories; all those experiments playing with Bunsen burners and metals that fizzed and popped when they touched water; all those chemicals that reacted in bizarre ways when mixed with other chemicals; all those odorless and tasteless hazardous chemicals; all those exciting possibilities. Mr. Johnson, the lanky Physics and Chemistry teacher was very careful when he portioned out the pupil's rations; these were dangerous materials they were working with. Copper sulfate crystals would be distributed in tiny measures with clear warnings not to ingest them in even the minutest amount. And so the plan was formulated. And slowly the stockpile of the blue crystals grew, sneaked out one or two at a time wrapped in tiny strips of aluminium foil. Finally the day came; Xavier was ready. He was going to go through with this. It was the only way that he would regain his freedom. At home one

Thursday lunch time (Jodie taught music on Thursdays at Durham Girls' School), his arm aching and bruised as usual, alone in the kitchen, Xavier made a thick, deep blue paste by dissolving the copper sulfate crystals in a tiny amount of water. He spread the paste on all four pieces of bread and then heaped on an extra thick layer of smooth peanut butter and finally a generous layer of strawberry jam. Xavier was shaking all over as he wrapped the two sandwiches in cling film and sat down to wait until it was time to leave, the anticipation of his imminent freedom streaming through his veins like cocaine. Walking briskly up Redhills bank, his thighs burning from the build up of lactic acid in his quadriceps, Xavier could feel his freedom getting closer and closer with each stride. This was the last day of his incarceration, never again would he live in fear of a beating from The Hunchback. He was going to be free! He made it back to school in record time, surprising even himself. He quickly searched out Ian in the school yard, spotting his hulking figure amongst the hoards of pupils all dressed identically, kicking footballs, throwing tennis balls, loitering, or sitting in small groups playing cards. A momentary pang of fear – not an internal questioning of morals and ethics, whether what he was about to do was right or wrong, but a fear that The Hunchback wouldn't eat the sandwiches and his plan would fail – this short-lived fear immobilized Xavier, but gritting his teeth, he shook it off and marched over to The Hunchback and his cohorts.

"Fuckin' 'ell! You sweaty bastard! Oh, Pally, look at this wanker! Looks like 'ees been shagging." Ian chuckled as Xavier approached.

"Ha, ha! I diven't think anybody'd fuck him like. Ugly twat!"

This sent the whole group in fits of wild laughter, a couple of them bent over clutching their sides.

Feeling strangely braver than he'd ever remembered feeling before, Xavier handed the neatly wrapped package to The Hunchback. He could feel sweat running down his back.

"Here you are Ian: two peanut butter and jam sandwiches." Xavier's voice was calm.

The Hunchback reached out an over-sized hand and grabbed the food. "Ta. Now fuck off!" He snorted like a pig, clearing his nasal passages of phlegm and spat, but Xavier had turned too quickly and so the undulating ball of yellowish mucus missed his shoulder by a whisker, landing on the gray tarmac of the playground with a 'splat!' Xavier wiped the sweat from his brow with his sleeve and walked off to look for Arash, the only other foreign pupil at Johnston and his sole friend at the school. "Wanker!" He mumbled quietly, making sure he wasn't heard.

That afternoon, leaving the Geography classroom, Xavier watched The Hunchback push through the bottleneck at the door and head off down the corridor to his Woodwork class. "Bye Ian," he said under his breath.

Two weeks later, when Ian Cummings finally returned to school, at the beginning of French, he swapped seats with someone on the other side of the classroom and from that day on, never once hit Xavier or asked him to make him peanut butter and strawberry jam sandwiches. Even though Xavier kept telling himself that his mission had been accomplished, a voice deep inside kept whispering, 'I should have used more. I should have waited until I had more crystals.'

Looking at this kind of behavior from a relatively detached perspective, one might think that we're witnessing the development of a psychopathic mind, someone that is a danger to society. We can analyze Xavier's behavior until the cows come home, reading into it all kinds of things, interpreting it this way or that way, demand that justice be done. We are all too willing to act as if we are entitled to pass judgment on those around us. But wait: the story has not ended yet and as we are about to see, Xavier's life was to become far from free, with a great deal more than just his liberty threatened. As contrived as it may appear, there was never the faintest idea in Xavier's head that he could possibly be exonerated for his sometimes cruel and oftentimes thoughtless actions, conduct that was completely lacking in any kind of sympathy or warmth; he knew he had done wrong; accepted that he had at times acted without a conscience. Albert and Jodie were both God-fearing Christians and had raised Denzil and Xavier in the same religious milieu that they existed in. For thousands of years, mankind in every culture has placed his faith in something spiritual, finding solace in the worship of one kind of deity or another. The appeasing of the gods was fundamental, paramount to a long, healthy and prosperous life. Xavier, following this episode, was to realize that perhaps some of the things he had decided to do, some of the paths he had taken, some of the things he hadn't done when he should have were going to come back around and haunt him continually. Fate. Karma. Call it what you will. There had been too much bad energy flowing out of him for life to continue normally any more. His survival was now in the hands of the gods. However, even after this is all said and done, realizing something as profound as this, grasping the significance of actions and acting upon this realization, learning to behave in a more suitable, correct manner are two separate and entirely contrasted entities. Most people are adept at bettering themselves through an epiphany such as this; not all though.

Chuck E. Cheese's would be that last place anyone would imagine being robbed by two armed men. At least that was what Xavier believed. Restaurant management is not the safest career, but it has its rewards – we're not here to go into those at this time, and probably not at all in this story. Albert had always wondered why Xavier had continued along this path rather than developing and using

227

his mind more effectively. The long hours, late nights and stressful environment that their son was subjecting himself to year after year worried both Albert and Jodie. The couple of years that he had worked at the Sahara Restaurant in Burlingame had been horrific; the threat of robbery constantly overshadowing Xavier's work days. Driving to the bank one Sunday morning with $14,000 in a plastic deposit bag in his lap, Xavier had been scared out of his skin when a silver van with tinted windows had screeched to a halt, its tires smoking, next to his Cadillac at some traffic lights and the passenger, a tattooed skinhead with a cigarette hanging from his lips leaned out of the window and shouted to him, "Hey fucker, get out of the car!" The lights had changed and the van had shot off.

There's nothing that you can do to prepare yourself for the moment when you are robbed at gun-point; no mental "exercises" to ready the psyche; no books that you can read that might make an armed robbery something that you can deal with; you simply either live through it and deal with it for the rest of your life. Or you die. Now, with all due respect, Chuck E. Cheese's did pay for Xavier to see a Psychologist for a couple of months and gave him three months paid leave following the robbery, but unless you are an emotional loggerhead, unless you are completely lacking any sort of sensitivity (and I hear you saying, "well look at Xavier, he tried to kill someone without a glimmer or remorse", and I say in his defense, "at that time in his life he believed absolutely that there was no other way out of that situation") unless you are an impassive moron, your life will be irrevocably changed after being robbed at gunpoint. Trust me on this.

To Xavier at least, looking back at it, as he did frequently until he eventually managed to file the incident away, safely concealed in his archives, the circumstances that led up to the robbery were suspicious. The last person to exit had been the General Manager's favorite employee, Gary Matthews, a seventeen year old stocky Jewish kid with a large mop of frizzy, light brown hair, even though Xavier had given him explicit instructions to wait while he had done his final walk-through of the restaurant. It was a Saturday night and as usual, the restaurant had been extremely busy all day, the employees all worn out and so the clean up had taken a while. Gary had arrogantly ignored Xavier's order and left through the front doors, leaving one ajar. Xavier had brought the fault in the door's self-locking mechanism to the attention of the GM when he had first noticed it some weeks earlier. Nothing had been done about it and so unless you pushed the door closed, it would remain ajar. Thinking that Gary was still in the lobby, Xavier had been thorough in his walk-though of the kitchen areas, checking that the close would be to the GM's satisfaction when he opened the following morning. Having completed his inspection of the rear of the restaurant, Xavier turned off the lights in the back and made his way to the front, still brightly illuminated. Seeing no sign of Gary, he called his name a couple of times, starting to worry. Hoping that the kid was in the bathroom but fearing that he wasn't, Xavier began hurrying. Everything looked fine at the registers. Before he could make his way around the front counter however, he heard the front doors move and turning to see who was coming or going, saw two black men pulling ski masks over their faces running towards him. They each had a gun drawn by the time they reached Xavier, one of the men leaping over the low counter with amazing agility and putting his gun against Xavier's temple. 'This is a joke!' was Xavier's initial reaction, formed by his brain in an attempt to dispel the terror. A sharp blow to the back of his head from the other man who was now also at his side and Xavier quickly began to realize that this was unfortunately no joke. Forced into the manager's office with a gun pressing into the middle of his back, Xavier was told to open the safe. Only just managing to get the words out, tears threatening to burst from his closed eyes, he explained that the safe had a fifteen minute delay timer fitted.

"Open the fucker!" one gunman yelled. Xavier dialed the combination on the keypad, his hand trembling like jelly. Two short beeps followed by a longer, single beep indicated that the timer had begun. One of the gunmen stayed with him in the office to wait, instructing Xavier to remain kneeling in front of the safe with his head bowed, arms at his sides. He kept his gun pressed against the back of Xavier's head.

"You turn around, I'll shoot you fucker!"

The other man disappeared and Xavier heard him scavenging around, knocking things over in the darkness. Xavier shut his eyes tightly, like a child, like someone practicing magic. If he closed his eyes tightly enough; if he couldn't see anything, if he pretended to know nothing, then nothing might happen; the men who had come in to the restaurant might both just go away.

The second hand on Xavier's watch ticked slowly, loudly, the sound seemed to be emanating from all around him in the small office; his heartbeat echoing off the walls.

"You got kids?" The gunman's voice made Xavier jump.

"A son."

"You wanna see him again, don't do nothing stupid." He paused for a while. The seconds ticked by slowly. The safe beeped intermittently. Xavier pictured Oliver without a father; not the way his life was now with his father no longer at home (once again), a father who came to visit every few days, who took him to the park or played with him in the pool, but as a young man who had grown up without a father; a young man whose father had been shot in the head by robbers.

"I'm sorry it's you man, it had to somebody right? I need the money." Perhaps a trace of compassion was developing in this man with the silver gun.

Xavier, for a brief moment thought that maybe the man was going to take the gun away from the back of his head. He felt the end of the barrel scraping against his scalp.

"Keep yer head down mother fucker!"

It seemed to Xavier that time was slowing down; the beeps from the safe were getting further apart; the second hand on his watch was dragging: T – I – C – K   T – O – C –K.

"You better not be fuckin' with me!" The gunman was getting restless. The sound of footsteps could be heard approaching and then the accomplice banged loudly on the office door. The gun stayed attached to the back of Xavier's head as the gunman opened the door.

"There's money in those white machines right?"

Xavier knew that the man was referring to the two bill changers – automated game token dispensers that did indeed contain, after an average Saturday, around $500 each.

"Where's the keys fucker!"

"Hanging on the wall behind the door."

The accomplice grabbed the string with a single key hanging from a screw and left. There was silence for a minute and then the man's heavy footsteps on the tile floor of the kitchen area and his angry mumbling could be heard getting closer followed by a loud knock on the office door.

"You open the mother fuckers!"

Xavier had been anticipating this: the locks on the bill changers were tricky to open, even for him.

"How long till the safe is open?"

Xavier opened his eyes and looked at his watch

"Don't turn around or you're dead!"

"Six minutes."

The gunman lifted the gun away from the back of Xavier's head. "Put that bag on his head."

There was a pile of cloth game token bags, the same kind that Banks use, against the wall to Xavier's left. Glancing quickly, Xavier caught a glimpse of the accomplice's arm and his small hand, which had a dark woolen glove on it as the man reached for one of the bags. A moment later the bag was pulled roughly over his head shutting out the light and making breathing difficult. The cloth smelt moldy.

"Get up!"

Xavier was almost pulled to his feet and pushed out of the office, his shoulder catching the doorframe with a dull thud. The man behind him guided him through the kitchen and out into the front of the restaurant that was still brightly illuminated. In this light, Xavier could make out the vague outlines of booths to his left and the two bill changers flanking the hallway that led to the front doors. The man guiding him grabbed the back of his shirt that had been stuck to his back. The bag was yanked off his head in one swift motion. Xavier shut his eyes to shield them from the glare of the ceiling lights.

"Put the money in the bag. I'm gonna be right here. You try anything and I will fuckin' shoot you!" With that the gunman pushed him towards the bill changers.

Xavier, in the deathly silence, for the first time noticed the soft "fump" sound that his feet made on the thick, hardwearing carpet.

'This is it! Run! You have to do it. They'll shoot you anyway after they've got the money from the safe.' Xavier set his teeth and took a deep, empowering breath.

"I'm right here!" The voice from behind him was low and full of strength.

As Xavier walked, he fixed his eyes on one of the orange-yellow pole lamps in the empty parking lot outside. It was raining slightly; the black tarmac glistening. Outside, merely twenty feet or so away, he would be free. Outside those double doors no one would be pointing a gun at him.

Xavier's fingers fumbled with the key that the accomplice had abandoned in the lock of the bill changer on the left. He managed to open it on his first attempt, the handle turned with a solid "clunck" and he lifted the heavy door up and then emptied the stacks of one and five dollar bills into the bag. He carefully lowered the door and walked over to the second machine. Out of the corner of his eye he could see one of the gunmen squatting down behind the soda fountains, the silver barrel of his gun glinting as it followed him.

The second lock proved to be more reluctant to open. Holding the bag under his arm, Xavier used both hands to try and turn the long, narrow key. It snapped suddenly.

"The key's broken." He wanted to cry; wanted to set free the tears that were pushing hard behind his eyes.

"Leave it! Get back here!"

As he approached the soda fountain, he could hear the gunman's feet shuffling on the tile. It was dark around the corner and in the darkness, he saw a gloved hand reach out and take hold of his arm, dragging him out of the light.

Back on his knees on the cold tile floor of the office, Xavier, his eyes closed, tears breaking through his eyelids, prayed to God for the first time in years. 'I'm sorry Lord. I know I've done a lot of bad things, please forgive me. Oliver doesn't deserve to lose his father. He hasn't done anything wrong.' The gun was again pushed against the back of his head. Time trickled on. There were five short beeps followed by a long beep and the gun lifted away. Xavier opened his eyes and blinked away the tears. He heard a voice but paid no attention to it – the end to this horror story was close. His heart was racing as he turned the heavy steel handle and opened the safe.

"Put it in the bags!" One of the gunmen kicked the pile of cloth bags, knocking a couple of them close to Xavier's knee. The man was wearing a blue Nike sports shoe with a mid-gray sole; it was fairly new and clean. He also had on black jeans. Xavier pictured himself picking out the man in a Police line-up: 'Yes, that's him. The one with the Nikes and black jeans on!'

Once the safe had been emptied and the two bags he'd filled had been grabbed by the small, gloved hand, Xavier felt a gun press hard against the back of his skull again. He

235

was told to get up and back out of the office. He was pulled backwards by his shirt, almost tripping over his heels a couple of times as he watched the office door closing. He heard the rear emergency door alarm go off close behind him and then he was turned around and pushed outside in the back lane. The only light came from a useless, dim security lamp high up on the wall to the left. It had stopped raining.

This was the first time Xavier had faced the two gunmen since they had first stormed into the restaurant. He looked at their eyes as they stood for a split second, getting their bearings. The shorter man with the small, woolen-gloved hands spoke first, splintering the surreal silence.

"This way!" He looked at Xavier; it was too dark for Xavier to determine what kind of look he had in his eyes that peeped through the narrow slit of the ski mask. His skin was as black as the wool; his eyes and their sockets looked like pools of oil. He blinked, the movement like a ripple, turned and then broke off running.

The other man, about the same height as Xavier, raised his silver gun as if in slow motion. He placed it against Xavier's forehead. The barrel looked shorter and thicker from this angle; the man's hand, in a black leather glove was enormous. Xavier looked into his eyes, not as dark as the accomplice's, but gave Xavier the impression that he was looking at black steel.

"You turn and you run!"

It was a simple direction. It left no question as to just what was required of him. 'You turn and you run' echoed in Xavier's mind as he considered what was about to happen. Time abruptly froze. Xavier pictured the scene from a bird's eye view: he saw the shorter, blacker man running towards the corner of the strip mall that Chuck E. Cheese's was in; watched as he himself turned away from the man who had a silver gun raised, pointing at him; held his breath as he ran, slowly at first, waiting for the shot, and then faster and faster as the distance between he and the gunman grew. He was running for his life. If he could only make it to the bend in the wall, get around the corner, he would be safe, but each stride he took seemed to make no difference. It was as though he was running on a treadmill. He heard two shots in his head and closed his eyes in readiness. And then all he could hear was his own panting; the only thing he could feel was the pounding of a heart; his heart; beating. He looked up and saw that he was around the corner, out of site of the back door, safe, alive.

Xavier thought that perhaps Katie, feeling sorry for him, having some compassion left in her heart, would delay the divorce proceedings. He wasn't sure why it was he didn't want to be divorced, it wasn't as though he was about to give up the girlfriends or the nights out drinking with the boys; pride perhaps; a reluctance to accept that he'd failed at yet another 'venture'. Katie however, didn't feel any sympathy whatsoever. On the contrary, her reaction, when

Xavier came to the house two days after the robbery to tell her about it, threw Xavier for a loop.

"Did you steal the money?" She was serious. Speechless for a few moments, Xavier realized that his marriage was over. The meeting with the mediator was a few weeks later, followed a couple of weeks after that by the visit to the courthouse. Both he and Katie wept as their marriage was annulled and Oliver's family unit was shattered for good.

Chapter 23: For whom the bell tolls

As the bright orange peel came away from the plump, juicy segments of the tangerine, the zest spraying into my palm and down my fingers, I looked up looked up at Xavier, a smile stretched wide across his face, his eyes mischievous, sitting in front of the window. He was holding a teaspoon over his mug of coffee daintily between his thumb and forefinger as one would hold a dart. His eyes caught mine and his expression hardened ever so slightly, as though he was unsure of how to gauge my curiosity. The aroma of fresh toast drifted in from the kitchen on a wave of warm air as Denzil swung the door open and entered the dining room. He was still dressed in his pyjamas and wiping sleep from his eyes.

"Who's up for a walk this morning?" His voice was lighter than usual. "Mummy's going to make some sandwiches if we're all going."

"Xavier?" Enquiringly, I looked again at his beaming blue eyes.

"Why not? Where should we go? We could drive up to Muir Woods."

"We could, I'm sure Jodie would like to visit them again. Denzil, ask her if she'd like that."

Denzil ambled back into the kitchen, yawning earnestly. (It always seemed to take Denzil a while to wake up; it wasn't that he was lazy or stayed up later than everyone else, he was simply an inordinately deep sleeper who could sleep through a doorbell or telephone ringing; he wouldn't be disturbed by the sounds of a world waking up around him, and the whole waking process seemed to be more drawn out, extended, than for most other people. But it had been discovered only recently that his slumber appeared to be controlled by light – leave Denzil in a dark room and he could sleep all day; turn on a light or draw apart the curtains and his eyes would open almost instantly. From that point on however, a great deal of time had to pass before he would be up for any kind of activity.) And so he ambled into the kitchen, the door closing gently behind him. I heard Xavier moving his chair away from the dining table, the plastic tips on the chair legs gliding quietly across the polished wood floor – the original Victorian floor, sanded, buffed, re-sanded and rebuffed, stained, sealed and finally polished to a high gloss – and as I turned, he came behind me, placing his hands on my shoulders.

"Daddy, thank you for everything you've done." He leant down, surprising me with a tender kiss on my right cheek. I placed my hands on top of his. I could feel the warmth emanating from his palms through the thin cotton of my shirt. A shadow swept across the dining room for a brief moment as a cloud drifted across the low but bright morning sun. I could see the fog beginning to break around the magnificent red towers of the bridge. Soon the whole structure would be clear of its early morning blanket, the shipping channel safe once more.

Jodie walked in as Xavier was about to speak.

"Muir Woods it is then?" She looked radiant: her cheeks glowing, her short, attractively graying hair brushed with subtle blonde highlights, her long, slender figure adorned with a beautiful pale yellow dress that she'd picked up in the Laura Ashley shop on Oxford Street in London the day before we left for San Francisco. Her elegance was reaffirmed by the delicate perfume that she was wearing which, as she approached me roused my senses and I felt my eyes widen. Xavier walked from behind me and met her with an embrace; I caught a glimpse of her smile as she squeezed him tightly.

"We could stop in Sausilito on the way back for tea or dinner, depending how long we spend at the Woods. What was the name of that place we had tea and scones at?"

Xavier released Jodi who, reluctantly relinquishing the embrace, began clearing the table.

"Tea and Sympathy, like the one in New York that I gave you the recipe book from, remember? Here Mummy, sit down, I'll do that." Xavier pulled out a chair for her and took the two plates from her hands. "I insist."

"Anyone for more coffee," Denzil's voice boomed from the kitchen. "I'm going to make a fresh pot."

We adjourned to the grand living room – grand in appearance and grand in ambience; the kind of room that when you first walk in through one of the tall, heavy doors (themselves quite grand) from either the living room or the hall, your breath is taken away as you take in the high, ornately plastered ceiling with the Italian crystal chandelier hanging regally from the center, the stately Brazilian slate fireplace, and you feel yourself wanting to utter something, some kind of exclamation, "Wow" or "phew", as though you had just come upon some lost treasure – adjourning to this grand living room, we relaxed with mugs of freshly ground Kenyan coffee and outlined our itinerary as the Golden Gate Bridge arose from her repose, creaking and groaning as she tightened her massive, wound oxidized steel cables in readiness for another day. Denzil was at last coming to life: his batteries no doubt charged with the rapture that this family reunion – the first in over fifteen years (life had isolated us from one-another for too long) – was bringing to us all. It felt as if we were all plugged into an electrical outlet, the elation rising within us all, clearly visible if you looked at our eyes, gleaming like gemstones, the very air around us filled with exultation. I could feel my head spinning, my scalp tingling as I watched the spectacle from a distance, removed in an out-of-body way, hearing my own voice (the languidness that had coated it for years now vanished), inhaling the glorious aroma of Kenyan coffee, watching Jodie's skittish movements as she took it all in from the armchair by the fireplace: the boys, successful adults, established in their fields, entertaining us, their aging parents in a joyous celebration of family, of life. (It wasn't until later that I contemplated the odd absence of the boys' own families: at this time, this point in my life, this was precisely how it was supposed to be; there was nothing missing at all; everything was as it should have been.)

The room began to spin faster and I felt a sensation of falling. For a moment, it was exhilarating, enjoyable, devoid of danger, like being on a fairground ride safely strapped into your seat. The moment passed or rather, receded. I could hear a rattling sound; a cracking or splintering or sawing of wood. The room was darkening; my heart beating harder, straining; the aroma of coffee was fading, metamorphosing into an odor of something peculiarly familiar; I couldn't place it at first, an unpleasant mustiness and the pungency of over-ripe fruit perhaps; or vegetables. Yes, that was it: vegetables; not one in particular, but more of a general, all-encompassing organic, vegetable smell, the kind you would imagine permeating your clothes as you walked around a hot and humid vegetable market in the tropics – one like the market in Kumasi on a sticky Saturday afternoon during the rainy season; the usually very fat women, their jeweled heads and bulging bodies wrapped in beautiful and brightly colored hand-woven kente cloth, seated on large, overturned aluminium buckets or sturdy wooden boxes (the type used for shipping fruits and vegetables), announcing the produce they had for sale along with the exceedingly low price they were selling it for with ear-piercing cries – it was that sort of smell. From somewhere beyond my consciousness, a pain began registering; it was as though someone else was describing it to me; I wasn't experiencing it first-hand, it was more of an idea, the anthropomorphism of a pain. It seemed to take a while for the grand living room with its high, ornately plastered ceiling, Italian crystal chandelier hanging regally from the center and the stately Brazilian slate fireplace to fade completely, disappear into a thick, gray fog. The bridge was gone too; it was as though they had never been, had never existed. The sound I had heard was rising fast to amazing crepitation. I could hear a voice but not one that I recognized at first. The voice became clearer; I could distinguish the intonations. Was I in England? London. South London? The Doctor!

Jodie listened, her face turning green, as Doctor Martin explained the procedures for the cleaning and dressing of Albert's finger.

"Now, it's going to be painful for a few weeks, but as it heals, you'll see the skin thickening over the tip, purple to pink. The gangrene has been completely removed so don't worry, there's no danger of it coming back as long as you keep it clean. I cut it well past the first knuckle to make sure we got it all."

Jodie swallowed hard and cleared her throat. "When will he be able to use the finger again? He writes a great deal." She paused to swallow again. "I'm sure he'll learn to use his right hand, but it'll take some time."

"It's hard to say. I'm sorry I can't be more specific, but with his poor circulation...the pills I'll give him will help so make sure he takes them regularly, won't you. He isn't getting any younger."

Behind his fancy glasses, his thin wire framed rectangular glasses, the doctor raised his eyebrows, his small brown eyes looking like buttons, as he made this last statement. The tone of his voice and even the way he carried himself, the haughtiness of his manner – he had a fakeness about him, a kind of practiced sophistication that comes from years of trying to fit in to a group, an environment that one was not raised to be a part of; a class above one's own – his supercilious manner was getting under Jodie's skin. This new encumbrance on their lives was going to be a strain on their already oppressive existence. It wasn't enough that daily life was like a vicious game of Russian roulette, dealing with the constant threat of robbery, carjackings, trying to carve out a life in this God-forsaken ruin of a country, but here was this obnoxious doctor, with his horrid Cockney accent, implying that her currently sedated husband who had just had the diseased end of his left index finger removed was decrepit and senile.

Two months after the amputation, Albert's finger was still showing little sign of healing. The skin had grown over the tip as the doctor had predicted, but the pills weren't improving Albert's circulation to any discernable degree. His hands, the fingers particularly, constantly felt cold and numb. He wore gloves whenever he could, but even the slightest brush against his recuperating finger made him wince in pain and so even that feat took a huge amount of resolve to accomplish. Learning to use his right hand was harder than he'd imagined it would be: mealtimes, bathroom visits, writing; all these essential daily activities had to be re-learned. He easily became frustrated; the pain in his finger never actually going away, even under the increased dosage of morphine, not quite an incapacitating pain, but more an annoyance like a lingering hangover. If it hadn't been for the warm December weather, things could have been a great deal worse.

"I hope it won't be too bad when we get to England. A week of cold weather's not going to help." Albert wasn't looking forward to the trip to England; had it not been for the fact that he had an appointment to see a doctor in London (one who didn't sound as though she'd been anything but a doctor in her professional life) who had voiced her concerns over the phone that Albert's finger wasn't healing as quickly as it should have been and that he and Jodie were going to stay with Xavier and his new girlfriend Debbie in Tampa and then travel on to El Salvador to visit Denzil and Sophia and the boys, he may have been inclined to stay in Zimbabwe for Christmas. They were leaving in a couple of weeks and Jodie was looking forward to escaping for a month.

"What's the weather going to be like in Florida? Have you checked your email recently to see if there's anything from the boys?" Jodie had been Albert's nurse, chauffeur, physical and mental therapist, tutor and mentor for the last two months and knew well enough that it had been over three weeks since they'd last sent an email to Denzil and Xavier – at 'CyberCafe' in Bulawayo, the newest of the internet cafés, Albert had helped her by dictating parts of it, in particular the itinerary for their Christmas Holiday – and that there was bound to be something from them by now.

"'This house really isn't very clean, what with two big, smelly dogs. I know that you'll be more comfortable in a hotel.'" Jodie stopped reading. The words were sickeningly familiar. She could hear Albert letting out a long sigh. She read a little more of Xavier's email, checking for content, before continuing aloud. "'I've found a couple of places not too far away that are quite reasonable, the links are at the bottom. If you have any problems booking somewhere, let me know and I'll look for some others.'" Jodie took off her reading glasses and turned to look at Albert. He looked so sad and tired; she wanted to say something to cheer him up but couldn't muster the strength within herself to be blithe. "Will we be able to afford a hotel. The one place he said was fifty dollars a night. How much will that be?"

With a heavy heart, Albert took a sheet of paper from the printer and began some rough calculations using his right hand, upsetting himself with his untidy attempts at numbers. He shook his head. 'Why couldn't he remain in a relationship?' For well over a year, all Xavier had written about was Debbie this, Debbie that; the gainfully employed (she was the Assistant Director of a private tutoring school), pretty, petite, twenty-four year old Greek girl with a degree in Psychology. Her parents had coddled Oliver, accepting the child and his divorcee father into their arms gladly; her family were all looking forward to finally meeting he and Jodie; things were finally looking up for Xavier following the spirit and soul-crushing effect of the divorce; and now this! An abrupt, unexplained end to the relationship – the fear of commitment no doubt – and their carefully budgeted travel plans had been thrown into disarray. 'What could it be that had given Xavier this weak character; made him utterly lacking in the conviction to be an adult, to take on and accept responsibilities? What was it that he and Jodie hadn't done while raising him?' As far as he could perceive, they had been there for him constantly, providing a safe, close and loving environment for him as he grew, fulfilling his every need, employing

248

full-time nannies to take care of him, showing him, by example, how to nurture and share love. Albert put his pencil down and awkwardly took off his glasses. Careful not to knock his thickly bandaged finger, he took out his handkerchief from his lapel pocket and began cleaning the lenses.

"Well," he sighed deeply again, "I suppose we'll just have to manage, somehow."

There seemed to be a system of doing things that Xavier had inherited through his father, a dream of glory together with a general pessimism, a wishing to hope and a nervousness about hoping. It made for temperament, frustration, self-destructiveness. It is as if we all carry in our makeup the effects of accidents that have befallen our ancestors, as if we are in many ways programmed before we are born, our lives half outlines for us. There was also the abyss; the vacancy in Jodie's heart, created or rather, never filled with love from her parents. Her childhood had been one full of loneliness, sadness and at times, despair; her father away for much of the time, her mother dying young, her step-mother ignoring her. It would take a whole other book to explain the pain that Jodie felt in her heart (perhaps after this tale is told, I shall set to work on that story). At this juncture however, the failure by her parents to offer her their love when she was a child only needs to be explained succinctly as it pertains to Xavier's life.

Children who are raised by busy working parents, as I have no doubt happens more so these days – now, I'm not going to go off into some 'psycho-babble' here, quoting studies, drawing charts to prove a point, this is merely an assumption of mine based on some brief studying on the subject of Sociology both in life and at college, but more importantly from first hand experience – these children of busy parents (busy on account of their excessive workloads or because they keep themselves occupied in order to avoid their children due to the fear they have of their unending clamoring, their neediness) are usually palmed off onto nannies. Weekend sojourns; short holidays away at the coast (usually to Elmina or Cape Coast) or in the mountains at Mampong or Amadzofe to the north; summer breaks traveling throughout Western Europe; these intervals of family unity, closeness, these precious times when Denzil and Xavier had their parents all to themselves became etched into the young boys' minds remaining as blessed memories for the remainder of their lives. These circumstances can be looked at two ways: Albert and Jodie were diligently forging out a life for themselves, the family, taking on workloads that would bring them great rewards (both financially and mentally) in order to have a lifestyle filled with luxuries and accolades but by doing so sacrificing the opportunity to personally shape the lives of their children; forsaking the joy of sharing first-hand, the day to day development of their children; alternatively, (through no fault of their own) Albert and Jodie simply didn't possess the necessary skills to cope with full-time parenting. It must be said at this juncture that most new parents who live in a place far removed from their own families, having no-one to help with the care-giving, often become overwhelmed by the rigors and tortures entailed in caring for a baby and would undoubtedly give anything to have a nanny take over now and then. In every society, it is commonplace to find children being looked after by someone other than a parent; there is nothing peculiar about this. Obviously, in an ideal world we would be able to raise our offspring ourselves and not have to leave them to the influences of people with a lesser concern for their well being and sociological development.

The fear of the unending neediness, the incessant clamoring of babies and young children can also easily be mutated, reprogrammed in the minds of parents so that looking back at those early stages of parenthood they can say without a shadow of doubt that the reason for relinquishing the opportunity to shape the mind of their child by spending as much time as possible with him or her was that they were simply too busy working to support the family; that there was no other way; c'est la vie. But, accepting that sacrifices have to be made somewhere, we do have a choice: Xavier was soon to discover that the guilt he felt for abandoning his son would continue to haunt him, grow inside his heart, his mind, his soul like a virus; tear at him to such an extent that he would eventually – by forfeiting creature comforts, giving up the idea of earning enough money to save for the future – chose a lifestyle that enabled him to spend a great deal of time with his son, as if by doing so he could make up for all the time he had missed, all the pain of not understanding that he had inflicted on his young and innocent son. At first this would be the only reason that Xavier could see for his change of heart, however, the more he thought about his inadequacies, his irresponsibility, he began to realize that there was also a burning desire inside him to ensure that his son did not turn out like him: lonely; emotionally estranged (and vacant) towards his parents; unable to commit his heart to one person; having to constantly search for love, attention and reassurance. The most horrible, cataclysmic thing he could do to his son was to condemn him to a life lived with an empty heart, a life full of unrequited love and tattered hopes. His son would not be like him. He was going to be there for Oliver, as his father, as his friend, as his guide.

Chapter 24: Dereliction

Ben was being his usual obstreperous self.

"Aye, niño! Cachetón, andáte pa' fuera y jugá con tu hermano, si no te voy dar un cinchazo." Denzil raised his arm to show the boy he meant business. Giggling maniacally, Ben dropped the plastic hammer that he'd been hitting the television with and walked over to the sofa where his father was lying and smacked Denzil playfully on the leg.

"Pappa, no sé donde está Antonio."

"Andá buscálo. Ha de estar por allá afuera." Denzil lifted his head and turned to look outside through the open door; the gate was also open. "Antonio! Antonio!" As his voice thundered in his head sending a pain bouncing back and forth, Denzil grimaced; last night had been worth it. With Sophia's mother staying with them, he and Sophia had gone out for the evening leaving the boys under the stern supervision of their abuela. A night out together! Such a rare treat it was: it seemed like the entire duration of their relationship had been filled with children; one baby after the other. Denzil wondered if 'Grandma' and 'Grandpa' would offer their services while they were visiting, and if they did, whether, even between the two of them, they would be able to cope with Ben – the younger Antonio was at the opposite end of the spectrum to his older brother; the two siblings bore no resemblance behaviorally, also Antonio's hair was much finer and wavy rather than thick and tightly curled as Ben's was; if it weren't for their matching, mesmerizing, pale brown eyes one might almost believe that they weren't related.

"Si Pappa?" Antonio was standing in the doorway smiling, a wet patch in the crotch of his denim shorts. Ben, seeing his brother's mishap, broke into a wild fit of laughter and fell back hard onto his bottom. Antonio, overly sensitive (sometimes to a girlish extreme) immediately started to cry. The noise that the two boys were making was demoralizing. Denzil's head wasn't ready for this cacophony.

"Sophia! ¿Vas a llevar afuera a los niños, porfa?"

With the house peaceful at last, Denzil stretched himself out and looked forward to a lazy afternoon dozing on the sofa. The glorious smell of pupusas cooking close-by drifted in through the open door on a relaxing, warm zephyr. How anyone could live in cold climates was beyond his comprehension; cold weather was neither good for the body nor the soul. He had suffered terribly during his years in the Police Force in Birmingham: bitterly cold, hateful winter nights spent patrolling the streets on foot, bundled up in his thick, black wool over-coat; the icy wind biting his nose and ears under the lip of his helmet, pulled down as low as possible; his breaths coming out in thick clouds; the diagonally falling sleet stinging his cheeks and chin. In the months following the move to Honduras, he had welcomed the tropical climate whole-heartedly, relishing the gloriously warm evenings during the winters like a child with a new toy.

A mosquito hummed annoyingly around his left ear; he pawed idly at it like a dog, catching a glimpse of the vampire out of the corner of his eye as it darted away up to the ceiling. Well aware that the mosquito was moving too quickly for him to catch it, he grabbed at the air as if to threaten it. As he reached up, the stretch marks that streaked along the inside of his upper arm emerged, twisting like rivulets from the sleeve of his shirt. The stretch marks – more like scars than marks – had come from the rapid growth that his (genetically predestined to be huge) arms had gone through when, in his early teens, he had taken up weight-lifting seriously. His chest and shoulders were also sliced with these pale scars. During his years of exercising he had left numerous training partners writhing in the gutter; fallen comrades who had been unable to keep up with the swift increases in his strength. He had quickly become feared at the gyms in Durham and had found it more and more difficult to cajole any one into training with him. He scratched at the stretch marks as he brought his arm down, flinching as the sharp edge of a nail caught one of his small, craterous, oval tumbu fly scars. 'Nasty buggers,' he said to himself as a minute trace of blood appeared. 'And you can keep off, you blood-sucking bastard,' he said to the stealthy, unseen mosquito that was humming somewhere close by.

During the rainy season in Ghana, the tumbu flies breed quickly in spite of the efforts to eradicate them by spraying pesticides everywhere. These insects are a menace to man and beast, laying their eggs in puddles (where thankfully the tadpoles devour them), wet grass (from where they get on to the skin of an animal), and oddly and most dangerous to man, in wet laundry hung out to dry (a careful and thorough ironing will take care of them however). The sticky, microscopic eggs, if and when they come into contact with the skin of an animal or man, adhere to their new home until the larvae hatch, whence they then immediately burrow down into the skin. From there, they grow into little, white, hairy maggots, which, if left to gestate fully, would emerge as fully developed tumbu flies within a couple of weeks. Treatment of furuncular myiasis is simple enough as there is no real danger to the 'carrier' of these larvae other than a minor infection localized under the skin that is easily treated through a course of antibiotics once the maggot (only when it had reached a certain size) has been relatively painlessly extracted.

As Denzil wiped the blood from the scar, a shudder rang up his spine as the memory of the 'popping day' flooded his thoughts. Looking back at that afternoon in Nhyaesu – he and Xavier standing sobbing and naked in the living room, the bucket of hot, steaming water ready to catch the emancipated maggots, the jar of Vaseline open on a towel on the piano stool, Albert and Jodie kneeling beside the two of them examining their numerous skin lesions – looking back at it now, the whole idea of it was ridiculous, comical. Denzil chuckled: suffocating little, white, hairy maggots that were growing under your skin, indeed! The first occasion that the tumbu flies had laid their eggs in the boys' laundry which had been hanging out to dry (Kofi, as was his system, always separated the boys' clothes from the rest of the laundry, washed and hung them on the washing line that stretched across the back garden and then folded the clothes neatly – he never ironed any items once they had dried as the chore of ironing was limited to Professor and Mrs. Lewis' clothes), this first time that the tumbu flies found the wet laundry was the last time that the boy's clothes didn't get a good ironing. Denzil only had thirteen lesions. Xavier, mysteriously had thirty-seven! Albert and Jodie, using one of Jodie's lesser-used lipsticks, marked all the lesions with an 'X' so they wouldn't miss any during the extraction process; the small bumps were to be found everywhere that the boys clothing had come into contact with – buttocks, upper thighs, torso, shoulders, chest, upper arms – and were becoming more itchy by the hour. Albert and Jodie then set to work covering each one with a thick coat of Vaseline. Once the boys had been checked over twice, everyone stood (or knelt) and waited. And waited. Denzil remembered he had been amazed at how long a tumbu fly maggot could hold its breath for. Suddenly one was spotted coming up for air, poking its tiny nose through the skin.

Albert had been given clear and precise instructions by a doctor at the hospital in Kumasi as to how best to perform the extraction (furuncular myiasis was a fairly common – and simple to deal with – problem in Ghana and so hospitals preferred that families handle it themselves rather than waste the doctors' time). One had to go round fairly swiftly, liberally applying Vaseline to the lesions in a circuit, being careful not to take too long as there was some pain involved which would no doubt make younger patients twist and writhe when the larvae were 'popped' out one by one, breaking the skin in search for air.

With the first little, white, hairy maggot out, the game had begun; Albert and Jodie and the boys scanned the lesions for any sign of a nose.

"Here's one," someone would cry.

"Ouch!" Plop: one little, white hairy maggot swimming in the bucket.

"And another!"

"OUCH!" Plop: two little, white, hairy maggots swimming in the bucket.

"Over here!"

"Ow! Ow! OW!" Plop: three little, white, hairy, maggots swimming in the bucket

Fifty plops, much squirming and many tears later, the game (not so fun a game any longer!) was over and everyone stood around the bucket watching the last of the little, white, hairy maggots drowning in the bucket of now warm water. The boys were put in the bath and scrubbed, rinsed, dried and then antibiotic cream was applied to the tiny, sore holes to prevent any infection. And now, as adults, the boys bear the small, craterous, oval scars as proudly as wounded soldiers back from war bear the scars of battle.

Smiling as the ambrosial aroma of pupusas wafted around him, Denzil rubbed his shaven head and closed his eyes; he was asleep within a few minutes, the devious mosquito settling softly on his ankle to enjoy its feast in peace.

At the house in Land O Lakes – the dirty house that smelled of dog urine, the dirty house on the nefarious, trash-lined street that was full of drug dealers and families on welfare, driveways littered with old, rusting Buicks and Pontiacs and Fords – Xavier bent over the kitchen counter once more, a tightly rolled dollar bill held to his right nostril, and inhaled sharply. The cocaine was hitting fast; three lines done with one more to go. This was such a great drug: you could drink a twelve pack during the afternoon, do a couple of lines in the evening and you'd be ready to go out. He had tried it once in England during his phase as a rock star in the band with Charlie but hadn't taken tried it again until a young and wild (temporary) girlfriend had re-introduced him to it recently. Xavier snorted up the last line, took a bump from the baggie with his car key for good measure and left for a night out with Josh at his favorite Irish pub. He reached the restaurant that his roommate was a manager at just as Josh was locking the front doors and the two of them sped off in Xavier's old, silver Nissan 300 ZX to drink some beer. As soon as they arrived at O'Hara's, Josh took the baggie from Xavier and disappeared into the men's room.

Life was good. Xavier couldn't keep still as he stood at the bar waiting to order; his feet tapping, his arms constantly stroking his head or scratching his bellybutton or checking his pockets. The air was filled with the smell of beer and cigarette smoke.
"A pint of Newcastle and a Bud Lite please Tessa." The bartender had such inviting breasts: not too big, not too small; they were clearly defined through the tight white tee shirt with 'O'Hara's' printed in bright red letters across it that she was wearing; one breast was perfectly ringed with the 'O', the nipple discernable just below the center.

"Four seventy-five please Xavier."

Realizing he had been caught staring at her chest, Xavier scratched his eye and blinked a few times, looking all around to make it appear as though he hadn't been staring, that he actually had something in his eye. Tessa took the seven dollars from Xavier and went off to claim her next victim.

"I'd love to fuck her," Xavier said as Josh appeared. Wiping his nose back and forth, he indicated to Josh that there was some cocaine visible around one of his nostrils.

"Gone?"

"Yep. A game of darts? Here, take the beers and I'll get the darts. Tessa, can I get some darts please darlin'? Hey Mike, how are you?"

Mike, the other bartender walked by nodding a hello to Xavier as Tessa sorted through the odd collection of darts, looking for the three that Xavier preferred.

Xavier could feel his nose tingling. He rubbed it hard. His eyes were open wide; he could feel the smoky air stinging them. His head was nodding in time to the Irish jig that the band was playing.

"Here you are."

Xavier took the darts from Tessa and pushed through the crowd, saying hello to each pretty girl he saw, towards the dartboards. This was the life: beer, cocaine, darts, a good friend, chasing women; what more could a man ask for?

His parents were arriving tomorrow. That would have prevented him from going out as much, made him cut back on his drinking and drug use had he not persuaded them to stay in a hotel for the week. It was going to be nice to see them, he had reminded himself during a period of sobriety (an afternoon perhaps), but the idea of calming down, even if only for a week, was not something he wanted to do. As it turned out, their presence didn't pacify him at all; he still managed to get drunk every night (even on Christmas Eve after work while they went to an Episcopal Church for Midnight Mass), showing up each morning at the hotel they were staying at just before noon (cocaine users tend to get to sleep very late), usually finding the two of them waiting patiently for him, reading or writing out postcards, sitting in the shade of the white painted wooden pagoda next to the pool. Occasionally he did feel guilty for his behavior, his tardiness, his lackadaisical attitude: he would speed dangerously through traffic, shifting gears hard, pushing the powerful Japanese sports car to its limits, swearing at slower drivers, projecting his guilt as anger onto whomever he could as he rushed to pick up Oliver en route from Land O Lakes to the hotel. But he could easily justify his actions. (I've forgotten what his reasoning was, but at the time I believe he did have his reasons. If you had asked him why his behavior was so bad, he would have given you a plausible explanation, I'm sure.)

The letter had been mailed from England – Albert had flown from Zimbabwe for his mother's funeral and had posted the family news update letters that Jodie had written from Gatwick Airport (he hand-delivered copies to his sisters) – arriving a week after Xavier had received the email telling of Grandma's death. He lay in bed, weak, still feeling nauseous, throwing up every couple of hours, unable to hold anything down, staring at the envelope on the green plastic table beside his bed. He reached out for it and carefully tore it open.

'…We had a lovely time visiting our sons in Tampa and El Salvador. Although Xavier had a busy work schedule, he was able to spend some part of each day with us, visiting Lowry Park Zoo one afternoon, Tarpon Springs another (we had some great photo opportunities on a sponge boat – Oliver with the diver, etc). We enjoyed a couple of wonderful meals at Bella's (the restaurant that Xavier is currently working at as head waiter); one with Katie and Alex (Katie's brother who is now living with her) and Oliver, and the other with Ana, a friend of Xavier's of Italian origin who is studying for her PhD at USF; a lovely young lady. It is amusing to see how adaptable Oliver is and how he obviously thrives on all the extra attention he gets. He worships Xavier, who is a very good father.'

Xavier put the letter down on the pillow and wiped the tears from his eyes. He lifted himself up and, gagging as his mouth filled with bile, staggered to the bathroom to vomit; traces of blood came up again. His stomach held nothing more than this disgusting bile; sour, yellow stomach acid that left a disgusting taste in his mouth. The six months of heavy drinking and smoking, an escalating cocaine habit and a poor diet had left him with tonsillitis, a stomach ulcer and sixteen pounds lighter. He struggled back into bed, avoiding the letter, and closed his eyes, painfully swallowing as he tried to wash away the dregs of the bile with a sip of strawberry flavored Gatorade. His eyes watered from the effort the vomiting took; his head pounded; he felt completely and utterly wretched.

Chapter 25: The End

'I wrote some thoughts down
on a piece of paper once
about a boy I used to know;
sent them off in a dream one night
hoping that by chance
that boy would come to see me.

Some years later I was alone
with only memories and tears
for the boy I used to know.
The sun had set on my future,
the darkness held my fears,
then suddenly that boy was here.

He had never once left me,
the whole time I'd been afraid
to open my eyes and see
that the little boy was me.
That lonely little boy was me.'

Xavier put the note pad back onto the bedside table. He felt a little better. He knew it was the medicine for his ulcer working and that in a couple of hours he'd be back to feeling nauseous and miserable. During his bouts of illness that re-occurred every year or so – tonsillitis had been a curse throughout his life, the doctors in Ghana at the time not convinced that removal of the tonsils would be of any benefit to the young boy – during these bouts of high fevers, an unbearably sore throat that made swallowing a hateful affair, and paralyzing headaches, Xavier, since the move to America, had pined for the attention of his mother; he wished for her to magically appear and sit on the bed beside him, stroke his hair tenderly, wipe his fevered brow with a cool, damp cloth, bring him yogurt and crushed banana. Katie had been a poor substitute (oftentimes men seek out the best qualities of their mothers in a partner and in doing so place an unfair burden upon their spouses) having been raised to be wary of men, to not become subservient, and over the years Xavier had grown to resent her for this maintaining of aloofness whenever he was suffering.

This pining that filled Xavier's heart arose from fanciful memories of his periods of illness in England (he remembered wishing that he could have been ill more often); episodes in his life when his mother had taken care of him herself; there had been no nannies to nurse him, no feelings of loneliness, separation, anxiety to compound the illness. Those years in Durham had been a learning experience for Jodie, an era of cognizance where she had to create, or rather, adapt the motherly nature that hadn't been fully developed in Ghana. Now, the fact that Xavier had very few memories of any childhood sickness, the fact that there were no clear memories of any periods of illness during his childhood in Kumasi led Xavier to assume that he must have been comforted and cared for (predominantly) by his nannies, even when he contracted malaria. It could be that the severity of that particular sickness erased any memory of it, the high fevers burning away the cells used for memory storage, but he had only the word of his parents recounting the horrific illness that had struck him at the age of seven or eight. (Xavier, looking back at his childhood in Ghana was able to recall the odd incident when he hadn't been looked after by his nannies: his recollection of the time, when he was five years old, that he cracked his head open at the Swiss lady's Kindergarten and his father had come from the University to pick him up was brief and naturally unpleasant. It wasn't unpleasant as a result of the pain, or because of the image he retained of standing in front of the pale wood framed, full length mirror in his parent's bed room staring at the open wound on his forehead that was bleeding profusely, blood running into his eye, or due to the eight stitches he had to have; it wasn't unpleasant for any of these reasons. The memory was unpleasant because of the anger he associated with it – not his own anger but that of his father.

There was an abruptness he could still feel now as a grown man looking back at the incident; a resentment almost, as though the injury had caused his father more discomfort and aggravation than it had him. Xavier recalled the impatience in his father's raised voice, his hurried attitude after he had picked him up from the Kindergarten and driven home – home to do what? This was a question that Xavier still dwelled upon: he remembered standing in front of the full-length mirror and his father making a phone call. Perhaps his father had been dragged away from an important meeting or some other pressing engagement, but the young boy, the injured boy clamoring for comfort, sympathy, empathy, love; this young boy, as the years passed and he slowly became an adult, remembered only that he had that day been nothing more than a burden that day; an unwelcome impediment in his father's important and busy life.)

There was a faint knock at the door; two light taps and then a single one.

"Yeah?"

"Xavier, how are you doing? Do you want to talk to Katie?" Josh opened the door and poked his head into the room. He looked genuinely concerned. At times, Xavier felt as though Josh was as close a friend as one could ask for, the kind that you could share your deepest secrets with. He had been good company at times, ready for a night out whenever Xavier wanted someone to carouse with. He had taken Xavier in when he first left Katie and again when he left Debbie. Xavier hadn't left the bedroom (other than to urinate or vomit) for over two weeks. His body was emaciated, his face pale and drawn, the sheets on the bed were fetid.

"I will, thank you."

Josh tiptoed in and handed the phone to Xavier.

"Hello, what is it?" he closed in eyes in preparation. He knew from experience that it was highly unlikely that Katie was going to offer her sympathies. Her soft voice was a shock.

"How are you feeling? Have you managed to eat anything." Xavier's first reaction was to contemplate what it could be that she wanted. Whenever Katie spoke with this delicate tone it usually led into some kind of request or another. Xavier could feel his scalp tightening.

"No, I can't hold anything down. I'm still throwing up every couple of hours."

"Are you up to having Oliver stay a night? He really misses you."

"I miss him too Katie, but I really don't think I can have him here. I haven't been out of bed in…"

Katie cut him off. "I need some child support Xavier." Her voice had in an instant lost every last trace of softness. "You have to give me something. I don't want to have to go to the court house." Xavier was at a loss as to what Katie had hoped to achieve by saying this.

"If I haven't been working how can I have any money to give you?" He was furious. How could she not understand the predicament that he was in?

"You need to pay…"

"Listen!" Xavier was shouting. The veins in his temples were throbbing painfully, making his eyes squint. His stomach was empty but still threatening him. "I haven't got any money to give you. Don't you understand? It's not as though I'm hoarding money here."

"Well, you better get back to work then, hadn't you?"

It was beyond belief that the woman on the other end of the line was the same woman he had at one point in his life been in love with. Marriage had been a catalyst for the gradual change in her sensibility; he knew that she had always felt the need to control his behavior, steer him in the direction that she wanted him to go and it had become obvious to him over the seven years they were married that the whole relationship had been led by her. He had lost his sense of fun, of freedom; his vibrant spirit had been quashed. The need for alcohol in his life was due in part to the frustration he felt, the feeling of being confined, stifled, trapped. When he was drunk he was free, he had his monkey-like energy again. If he hadn't come to America with her; if he had stayed in Key West when she wanted to leave just as his music career was taking off; hadn't married her merely to get his Green card; hadn't made love without a condom that night on the balcony under the stars in Burlingame; or if he had even tried to love Katie, love her for the beautiful person she was, how different life would be now! (He had been afforded so many opportunities to carve out a life that he wanted but instead had allowed his life to be led by Katie's dreams and had virtually given up on himself.) If, at any point during their time together, he had only had a clear vision of what he wanted from life, where would he be now? Where would the three of them be now? He only had himself to blame, but human nature does not usually allow us to berate ourselves too much; eventually we must take out our frustration on someone or something instead.

"Fuck off Katie! Just fuck off!" He cut off the call before she could respond. He lay on the bed, another fever coming on quickly. He had been advised not to take any more Ibuprofen as it would only aggravate his ulcer and so knew that he was in for a tough few hours unless he could get to sleep before the fever got too bad. Within seconds the phone was ringing. He silenced it and turned to face the wall. His skin was clammy. He felt alone, alienated, like he did when he was taken to live in England as a child.

There is a compelling part of human nature, one which is not rooted in bodily processes – the need to eat, drink and sleep, to protect oneself against enemies and so on – but in the very essence of the human mode and practice of life: the need to be related to the world outside oneself, the need to avoid aloneness. To feel completely alone and isolated leads to mental disintegration just as physical starvation leads to death. This relatedness to others is not the same as physical contact. One may be alone in a physical sense for many years and yet one may be related to ideas, values or at the very least social patterns. That gives one a feeling of communion and 'belonging'. On the other hand, one may live among people and yet be overcome with an utter feeling of isolation, the outcome of which, if it transcends a certain limit, is the state of insanity that schizophrenic disturbances represent. It was this lack of relatedness to values, symbols, patterns (which we can call moral aloneness – equally as intolerable as physical aloneness) that, had it not been for the faint memory of his beautiful son, his innocent, hurting son, threatened to draw Xavier down once more.

He awoke a few hours later with one page of the letter from his parents stuck to his left shoulder blade. The fever had subsided, draining itself onto the bed sheet and into the pillow. Xavier collected the pages of the letter together and, chewing his bottom lip, continued reading from where he had left off.

'The day after Boxing Day – very early in the morning, having said our good-byes the previous night – we drove down to Miami to catch the afternoon TACA flight to San Salvador. We were met by Denzil, Sophia and the two boys, both of whom were very shy at first, but once we had reached their home both came out of their shells. Ben is great fun, bouncing about like Tigger constantly whereas

Antonio is much more laid back. On New Year's Eve the Salvadorians celebrate the occasion with the loudest, most thunderous fireworks I have ever heard! We all stayed up until after 2am watching the wonderful displays.

Although we had little chance to relax, the warm weather and sightseeing were delightful and Albert's finger didn't cause him too much discomfort.

Upon our return to Bulawayo, we were horrified to learn that Samuel, our night watchman who was beaten by burglars recently had suffered permanent brain damage as a result of his injuries. The Police finally made an appearance at the house to take our statements and notified us of Samuel's condition. Albert was robbed again a few days ago in town by car-jackers whose modus operandi is to slash one of the tyres on the car after the owner has parked it somewhere and when the owner returns, a group of men will appear and offer to help replace the flat. They cause a commotion and during this, the car will be ransacked and the owner pick-pocketed. Albert had his wallet stolen again along with some valuable British currency and also his briefcase with his expensive pain and circulation medication inside. As usual, the Police have been useless.'

There is a point that we all come to along any given avenue, a particular path of life that we have been traveling along, heading towards a goal we had once set for ourselves when we must slow down, or perhaps even stop

273

to make sure that we are still facing in the right direction; ensure that our course hasn't been deviated. Throughout one's life there are obstacles, speed bumps and curves that one must negotiate. Pulling oneself back on track can be effortful and can make one rethink one's goal or objective. Lying in bed day after day, wretched and dolorous, contemplating his lot, his very existence, Xavier, through no conscious effort – in a way almost as extreme as a spiritual awakening; a true epiphany – began a new way of life. He had suddenly and without warning lost the desire to drink, lost his addiction to cigarettes; he no longer wanted to subject his organs to any kind of detrimental habits; he had truly turned over a new leaf. As time passed, days becoming weeks, weeks becoming months, Xavier began to look back at his life with a feeling of absolute disgust, antipathy; his new found enlightenment feeding his abhorrence toward himself. Now much more than ever he felt cast down, spending his time berating himself for the years he had wasted with self-aggrandizement, time which was lost forever, rather than commending his resolve and patting himself on the back for such a major accomplishment.

Xavier, attempting to validate his behavior, the self-importance he had lived his life within, had both his childhood and his mother's family history to look to for support. Of course the son of a white man in (post) colonial Africa would have a great life: his people had conquered this land. He was to a certain degree, as much as he tried to deny the fact – pointing to his half-African brother to corroborate his argument – racially prejudiced. However, if we try to classify Xavier's thinking we can see that this was not true colonialism – the ogre that enslaved people with darker skin because God had ordained that the white race was somehow superior. (The early colonists found it very easy to dismember the teachings of the Bible in the name of progress – the fact that the Africans had no knowledge of the white God meant that they obviously needed to be enslaved in order to ensure their redemption.) He was not discriminate in his prejudices however: the narrow-minded, bigamist people of the North-East of England; the self-centered, overly egotistical Americans; no-one was as virtuous or deserving as he was. He displayed a certain amount of tolerance and showed some affection towards anyone else who had been born and raised in Ghana or who displayed the same appreciation for the simple things in life as he himself had. In addition to this colonial grandeur that he felt he was a part of, there was a nobility, an aristocracy that occupied his head which, backed up by literature, he could prove ran proudly in his veins. Following the death of Jodie's great-aunt Lulu – her last remaining relative – Albert had done a great deal of research into Jodie's family history and uncovered a wealth of information. It was revealed that the sadness in Jodie's life was partly hereditary, running for generations and worsened by alcoholism that had been the cause, ultimately, of the expenditure of the family wealth. But, more importantly from Xavier's perspective, it turned out that she was a descendant of landed gentry, with ancestral homes in Scotland (a great castle overlooking Loch Ness) and in St. James' parish in Barbados (a house that was once part of a great sugarcane plantation established by one of her Scottish ancestors in the mid-eighteenth century). It was due to these two important factors in his life that the self-aggrandizement that Xavier had adopted from a very early age and projected onto anyone who was not a part of his Ghanaian image of Utopia – a multi-racial society of superior beings existing peacefully, contentedly in a fanciful garden of Eden – still lingered and continued to affect him in adulthood.

Chapter 26: Freedom (opus two)

'I'm waiting at the traffic lights,
waiting for the whole world to change.
Driving home along busy streets,
Driving home to my lonely room.'

If, twenty-four years earlier, Xavier could have been granted a glimpse of himself as being free, someone with no false and fragile attachments to the material world, he would have considered himself blessed. The blessing he felt as a blessing still; but – as with the pain that attends love – the disappointment that had come with the blessing he felt as a terrible solitude. Life was simple: that was what he had always wanted. But what a price he was paying!

The angry, impatient waiter finished taking their order. He had been standing over their table chewing his nails while waiting for them to decide what they were going to have. He wished the white people would leave his country. President Mugabe had said that the country rightfully belonged to the Africans; that the whites should leave.

'Why were they still everywhere?' He was going to spit in their soup.

"He wasn't very pleasant was he?" Jodie watched the man saunter across the empty dining room, his black trousers hanging low on his hips, and disappear into the kitchen. She turned to look at Albert. He was staring at a young black boy, twelve or thirteen years old perhaps, wearing the school uniform of the Northlea High School, who was standing on the pavement outside the restaurant, illuminated by a street light, making faces at him through the glass. Dusk was falling quickly, the sunset concealed by dark clouds. The boy was soaking wet; his white, short-sleeved shirt stuck to his body; his skin shone like polished mahogany. His green and white striped school tie hung down over his flat, bare chest and stomach; his shirt unbuttoned and open to his belly button. The black leather shoes on his feet were covered in mud. A number of private schools in Zimbabwe had recently been shut down for a few days after the government decided that their rate increases were illegal and racist; an attempt to drive out black students. Northlea had been one of those locked up by the police.

"He deserves a smack; cheeky boy!" Albert waved his hand as though brushing a fly away from food. The boy put his tongue on the glass and licked it before running off across the street laughing.

"He's just being a boy. That's what they do." Jodie feigned level-headedness and sensibility. She swallowed hard and took a sip from the glass of the room temperature water that the waiter had brought over when they had first sat down. She yearned for the genuine friendliness and the much more courteous behavior of the children in Ghana.

"Boys will be boys, I suppose you're going to say next." Albert smiled and took hold of Jodie's hand. "I remember when Xavier was growing up, how he could drive us to the end of our tethers. He was always getting up to mischief, coming home soaked to the skin."

The rain had started again, not as heavy as earlier, more like a English summer shower. The restaurant felt warm and cozy. The waiter returned with a bottle of house red wine, opened it effortlessly and poured out two glasses without offering Albert a taste. He placed the bottle down hard on the table and sauntered off again. A drop of wine ran down the outside of the bottle and onto the white cotton table cloth.

Albert's finger had healed fine and apart from the occasional tingling (his brain occasionally created an itch where his fingertip should have been) gave him no problems whatsoever. His circulation had eventually been improved by the medication that the Cockney doctor had prescribed. He had adapted his life to one without his primary index finger, preferring to ignore it completely rather than find uses for 'the stump', as he referred to it. Albert handed a glass of wine to Jodie and raised his own in a toast.

279

"Happy Birthday dear."

Their glasses clinked as the waiter approached carrying two bowls of soup. He placed them down carefully on the table.

"Deh bread is coming." He smiled politely and excused himself.

Jodie picked up her spoon and scooped some steaming creamy mushroom soup from the edge of the bowl. "So, are they going to let you know if they receive any applications?"

"The vice-chancellor promised to keep me informed. Obviously I'd have to screen anyone they were considering. Once someone's been chosen, I would have to spend a few weeks showing them the ropes."

Jodie had always admired Albert's resolve, his dedication to his work. Time and time again he had displayed this strength of character even under the most barbarous pressures. In Ghana, he had delayed the family's departure for the same reason as the escape from Zimbabwe was being postponed now. Even so, there was always a delicate balance between this dedication to his work and his devotion to his family that was conspicuous in the way he made sure no one was going to suffer. Work never came before family.

During the final year of Albert's contract, the post of Director of the Department of Architecture had been advertised worldwide but the University had had no inquiries. It seemed that the rest of the world viewed

Zimbabwe as too volatile and unstable, the President continuing to offer up displays of his neo-fascist dictatorship, turning the country into a veritable time bomb. Although Albert and Jodie felt safe at home now due to the recent organization of a neighborhood watch (with gun-totting vigilantes patrolling the streets), the news and mail was being censored, President Mugabe was trying to enforce a mandatory system-wide email monitoring system and the car-jackings (non-lethal as yet but very frightening none-the-less) continued unabated. The vice-chancellor of the University had offered Albert a substantial pay increase to stay in his post until such a time that a successor had been hired and trained. Albert had reasoned that if he did stay for one more year, he would be able to see his third class graduate. There was also the problem of securing another job before leaving this one.

The waiter returned with some slightly stale smelling warm bread. Basic commodities such as bread, fresh milk, butter, flour and rice were still hard to come by, but could be bought occasionally on the black market. Albert broke off a piece and offered it to Jodie. There was a softness, a warmth in her eyes, which Albert knew, came from a serenity she exuded whenever she felt safe and loved. He had seen the same look at some point during his overnight stay in hospital after the amputation; he couldn't remember when exactly. Perhaps when she had woken him in the morning.

"Look, he's back." Jodie was smiling back at the cheeky boy who had been making faces through the window at Albert. The rain was falling harder now. The boy was standing in the road watching them, laughing and pointing at them, large raindrops bouncing off his shaved head. Albert could barely hear his cackling over the music coming from the speaker in the ceiling above him.

"He's going to catch a cold, soaked like that." Jodie pulled her cardigan around her as a shiver ran up her spine.

"He looks like he's having fun. It's not that cold this evening."

The boy, seeing that he had an audience, continued his show with a lively dance routine. As the waiter was clearing the soup bowls, Albert saw a police car pull up silently, unnoticed behind the boy.

"Oh, he's in for it now. Look dear, they're…" He stopped talking as the car came to a halt.

Just as Jodie looked up, a thin, wiry policeman stepped out of the car and with one swift movement raised his black baton and brought it down on the back of the boy's head. Jodie jumped in her seat, gasping in disbelief. The boy fell to the ground clutching his head, his screams clearly audible to her, even through her tinnitus.

Albert got up in an instant and stormed out through the double glass doors into the cold, pouring rain. His shoes splashed water up inside his trouser legs as he stepped off the pavement into a large puddle. He reached the boy quickly and knelt down beside him. Blood was dripping from between his fingers onto the road, the rain washing the drops of red away as soon as they landed. Albert looked up at the policeman who was wiping his baton with a small white towel.

"Why did you do that? He was only having some fun." Without warning, the boy got to his feet and ran off across the street towards the row of shops opposite the restaurant still screaming and clutching the back of his head with one hand. In his haste, his green and white striped Northlea School tie fell from around his neck to the ground. Albert stood up, strands of wet hair sticking to his forehead, water running down his glasses.

"Go back inside. Dis is not your bisness. I know dis boy." Using his baton, the policeman pointed to boy who was now standing in the doorway of 'Chic', a woman's clothes shop, still clutching his head with one hand and defiantly shouting obscenities in Ndebele at the policeman. The policeman arrogantly cleared his throat and spat, just missing the boy. "Deh boy is always causing trouble."

Before Albert could speak, he got back into the police car and drove off after the boy, now running down the street towards the roundabout. Albert retrieved the tie and hurried back into the restaurant. The waiter, who had been standing inside watching, held the door open for him.

"Thank you. Did you see what happened?" Albert took his glasses off and began drying them with his handkerchief.

The waiter shook his head. "Deh boy is always coming here making mischief. He needs to learn a lesson."

"But he wasn't hurting anyone." Albert was still in a state of shock and complete disbelief. The waiter said nothing and walked off.

Back at the table, Jodie put her arms around Albert's wet shoulders, hugging him. She straightened his hair, kissed him lightly on the cheek and then took off her cardigan.

"Here, put this one till you warm up." She was insistent and he did feel a chill from his damp pullover.

"He was just having fun." He looked as though he was about to break into tears.

"I know dear. It's so sad. I hope he's alright." Jodie glanced down at Albert's hands. "Did you get any blood on your hands?"

Albert looked them over. "I don't see any. I'll go and wash them to make sure. I need to dry myself off a bit too." He stood up and headed for the bathrooms. Watching her husband, so tall and distinguished looking, with a lovely cream colored cardigan wrapped around his shoulders, his wet shoes making a squeaking noise as he walked, Jodie giggled suddenly. She hurriedly gulped some water to disguise her amusement. He was her hero, there was no doubt about that, but he could be quite clownish at times.

Xavier loved the rain. He loved the sound it made, loved the smell; the way the wind changed when it rained. In Florida, it rains like it does in Ghana. He and Oliver were waiting outside the Museum of Science and Industry for the Summer Camp teacher to arrive. They had got there early so that Oliver could finish his daily McDonald's Happy meal – he simply had to have the complete collection of toys! The rain was falling quietly, silently almost. Oliver was watching it entranced, his mouth full, chewing slowly. He looked at the rain as it began to fall harder, the raindrops landing heavily on the roof above them. Getting up from the picnic table, he walked out from under the shelter of the metal canopy and stood there, his little face pointing to the sky, laughing as the rain fell even harder, thundering now on the roof. From across the parking lot, parents hurried their children under gigantic umbrellas towards the shelter. Xavier watched, laughing as Oliver enjoyed this moment, this precious, fleeting moment that within a few years would have faded into a distant memory in his young, developing mind. Moments like these, however distant, we never forget. As he watched Oliver, Xavier saw himself, his clothes soaked, his fine, blonde hair (like Oliver's) messy and bedraggled, not caring how he looked or whether he'd catch a cold, standing in the rain and playing in the puddles in the driveway of the house in Nhyaesu, in a beautiful moment; remembered seeing his father watching him from the study, smiling, allowing him to be careless and free and just stand in the rain; letting him be a child and enjoy being a child. He saw himself being pounded by the rough surf attempting to show off his board skills to his father, standing watchfully on the beach in front of the chalets of Elmina Motel. He recalled his precarious baobab and mango tree climbing displays in the front garden, rewarded with fatherly praise. Xavier could feel the goose-bumps rising up on his arms and legs. The back of his scalp began tingling; his stomach tightened, a nauseous feeling briefly sweeping over him. As he lay on his bed, it appeared as though the whole room was being illuminated by a bright, blazing white light. The walls and the ceiling were almost blindingly white; it was like snow blindness – a condition that can cause a person to faint when they first step outside into a completely snow-covered landscape, a world too white and too bright for the brain to deal with. Xavier realized that he had been free all along, for his entire life. Never once though had he been free from love. Never once had his father tried to stop him from being free, from being what it is that a child is supposed to be, from being whatever kind of son he chose to be.

If we all had been given the chance to be children just a little while longer; if our parents had allowed us to enjoy what being a child is all about; if we could be children one more time, even if only for a moment, a fleeting, blissful moment, like standing in the rain with our faces turned to the sky, laughing, how much happier would we be? Are we not all too wrapped up in the way we look, the way we imagine people will judge our juvenile behavior? As adults, must we relegate our innocence, our euphoria, to fanciful memories? There is, I believe, in every one of us, a child crying out to be noticed, to be heard.

Chapter 27: Snow

Winter is finally here. A new-comer to the splendid world of a climate with four distinct seasons – clear and easily defined changes in the behavior of nature and the also the behavior of people – I am enamored by the winter season in particular. I remember the first time my father read one of his favorite poems by Louis MacNeice to me, the way the fine, blonde hairs on my early teenage arms stood up straight as the most beautiful winter scene I could imagine was laid forth before me in the words he was reading:

'The room was suddenly rich and the great bay-window was
spawning snow and pink roses against it
soundlessly collateral and incomparable:
World is suddener than we fancy it

World is crazier and more of it than we think,
incorrigibly plural. I peel and portion
a tangerine and spit the pips and feel
the drunkenness of things being various

And the fire flames sound with a bubbling sound for world
is more spiteful and gay than one supposes-
on the tongue on the eyes on the ears in the palms of one's
hands-
there is more than glass between the snow and the huge
roses.'

As he recited the poem, I imagined myself in a situation
not too dissimilar to the one I'm in now – sitting in front of
an old wooden desk, surrounded by books and papers in a
high-ceilinged study or living room, warm, safe and
contented, listening to an old, scratchy Simon and
Garfunkel record, gazing out through leaded windows at
the delicate snowflakes falling, like tiny white feathers,
onto the trees, the roof-tops, the hats and shoulders of
people outside my window – I felt the closeness, the love,
the connection between us prickling beneath my skin like
static electricity. He and I had been sitting on a bench at
the beach end of Golden Gate Park in San Francisco overlooking the ocean, the sun beginning to set, a warm, salty
breeze washing off the water. We had spent a wonderful
day together walking around the Haight-Ashbury district
and the park. Rummaging through the shelves and boxes of
books in a second-hand bookstore, he had excitedly picked
out an ancient and battered book of collected twentieth
century British poetry. Thumbing through the pages, dust
rising and falling around him in the dimly lit, musty

smelling store, he had opened the book close to the end, cleared his throat and began reading quietly. I had been just out of earshot but as I had moved closer he turned to look at me and told me how he had put this poem to music, composing a short piece of music on his guitar when he and my mother had first moved to America. His eyes had watered as he spoke; I could see the pain in his expression, the memory flooding his whole being, the past pulling at his heart. He had quickly paid for the book, the young Asian girl – a little older perhaps than I was at the time – at the register flirting with him, commenting on his (still very) British accent, and handed it, wrapped in a brown paper bag to me. "You'll enjoy these Oliver," he said to me, not letting go of the package. We had then walked out into the bright sunlight and set off to explore more of the delights that Haight-Ashbury held in store, the young Asian girl smiling at our backs.

Over the summer holidays that I spent with my father at his home in San Francisco, he would talk of his own summer holidays, particularly the ones in England as a child: the promise of a month or so spending precious time with his parents; the pure excitement, the unadulterated thrill of transcontinental air travel and all it entailed – watching the gigantic Ghana Airways DC10 aircraft with the Ghanaian flag resplendent on its tail, the intriguing Adinkra symbols decorating the interior, being loaded with baggage; the smell of the jet fuel as he climbed the tall stairs to the dark oblong doorway high above him at boarding; the always beautiful, elegant stewardesses in their prim, starched dresses; the almost frightening shuddering and heart-stopping acceleration at takeoff; the hypnotic humming of the engines during flight; the view of the world below (mostly the Sahara desert) from the window – this excitement, this absolute thrill of air travel had been passed on to me at a very early age. My mother's United Airlines flight benefits enabled her and me to travel easily around America and beyond during my earlier childhood years, going on many trips back and forth to England visiting her remaining family in and around County Durham. I also vaguely remember a short holiday she and I went on to Hawaii where I had first learnt to surf – a sport my father had enjoyed as a child in Ghana and had anxiously encouraged me to try whenever I had the opportunity. This thrill I still have, childlike almost, whenever I fly nowadays, always choosing a window seat, spending the entire flight with my face pressed against the plastic inner window, my eyes as wide and bright as silver dollars.

My father would speak of the joy he felt in his heart as a child reuniting with his big brother who was being educated at the imperial and prestigious Bembridge School on the Isle of White – a school with a world-wide reputation that drew pupils from many of the (former) British Colonies; pupils from a myriad of cultures and ethnic backgrounds; pupils who, like Denzil would be flown in, at first lonely and scared, but later, as the boys became more and more aware of their place in the world, confident and noble. The school's spring term ended with a great sports day – an occasion with the same atmosphere of the fair, of women's clothes, of bright colors and big hats, of normally demure but now gregarious, overly-proud parents; the same atmosphere of dressing up and showing off, the same atmosphere of a society especially mixed for the occasion; boys and masters showing off and ribbing with their fellows. Denzil had been a great athlete as a young man: my father often proudly spoke of the year he witnessed his brother, his hero, breaking the school records in the one and two hundred meter sprints, the long jump, the shot-putt and the discus.

I have no memory of the time I was presented to my great-grandmother during a visit to Suffolk – I was only a few months old – but knowing that we had met, and knowing that I would never get to meet her – she died peacefully of old age when I was six – I loved listening to my father as he spoke of the time over the summer holidays in England that he would spend at his grandparent's home in Ufford, a small and friendly, closely-knit village not far from Ipswich in Suffolk (the home designed and financed as a gift to his parents by my grandfather). He spoke of these holidays with an emptiness in his eyes – perhaps not an emptiness but more of a pining for a lost treasure. He so enjoyed the all too brief stays at this gorgeous house, on a gated street (one entered the street through a proud and regal stone gateway arched by an impressive name-plate with 'Ufford Place' in tall, decorative letters fashioned from black painted wrought iron); delighted in waking each morning to the aroma of fresh toast and the songs of sparrows and wood-pigeons; playing with his clownish grandfather in the large, carefully tended garden; hearing the strains of Scot Joplin or Chopin or Mozart (played on the grand piano by his mother or grandfather) wafting throughout the house and out of the living room windows on the light summer breeze; investigating his grandfather's fascinating tool shed and compost heap that were hidden from view by tall, neatly pruned box; exploring the mysterious, eerily quiet, shadowy woods (which, if the light was right, could be a little scary) that grew behind the house and down some way to a narrow brook with his brave, all-protecting brother; sailing the toy sailboats in the shallow river that the brook ran into after cascading over a small, stone weir; the freedom, the joie de vivre he felt, never restrained or confined but nevertheless always under the watchful eye of his father; the nightly bed-time stories (usually Hergé's *Adventures of Tintin* which, unavailable through the Puffin Club, would, during each summer holiday, be purchased in the better-stocked-than-Ghanaian bookstores in Ipswich), read with his father over and over again (I believe that my passion for literature was learned by my father's sharing with me of these fantastic books – I had in my possession by the age of nine, as he had done too, the entire collection). Although I never told my father of this when I was with him, feeling an odd shyness, embarrassment that plagues all of us as children perhaps, but each time I boarded the plane for the five-hour flight from Tampa to San Francisco, I would feel a lightheadedness, a feverishness almost, with butterflies prancing gaily inside my stomach as I imagined the oh-so-precious time we were about to spend together; pictured my arrival; saw myself running to him through the crowds of smiling or frowning or blank faced people; hugging him tightly, not wanting to let go of him.

If indeed there was a system of doing things that my father had inherited through his father, a dream of glory together with a general pessimism, a wishing to hope and a nervousness about hoping; if we truly do carry in our makeup the effects of accidents that have befallen our ancestors, as if we are in many ways programmed before we are born, our lives half outlined for us, then I must have missed out; the system must have failed. As I sit here at my desk in my room overlooking the courtyard of the college dorms, snow falling gently outside my window, my fellow students walking below, bundled up in warm overcoats, my soul mate sleeping peacefully in my bed, I look back at the childhood that my father bestowed upon me with a sense of joy I warrant you could not fathom. Although I have yet to visit his homeland with him – we have promised ourselves that once I have completed my studies, we shall spend some time traveling around Ghana, visit the home he grew up in, visit his Utopia – I have his stories, his tales; I have shared his joy, or rather, I should say he has shared his joy with me. I thank God and my grandparents for the love that they gave my father, the freedom they allowed him to exist in as a child. The summer of my fifteenth year, I flew over to Ireland to stay with my grandparents at their home – an idyllic restored farm cottage just outside Limerick. My grandfather still hadn't retired, teaching valiantly through his seventies, a man with a true passion for what he did. He talked at great length about the fears he had had for many years about my father's and also about his own future. The one thing that was apparent though throughout the long conversations we had was the deep, soul-binding love that he had for my grandmother, my uncle Denzil and my father (the ancient Greeks had a word for that kind of love, the kind of love that God has for mankind and also the self-sacrificing love they believed we should all have for each other – 'agape'). There is so much that we as human beings have yet to learn about life and love, about human nature, about freedom, but I absolutely believe that if we each took just a moment out of our hectic lives to look back at our childhood, look to the child within us, stand in the rain one more time with our little faces pointing to the sky, we would remember the freedom that we either were fortunate enough to be brought up within or wished for but never had, we would become more centered, more understanding. It is as simple as remembering that it is true what they say: wherever you go, there you are.

The End

(Ali, Deanna, Dawn, I am eternally thankful for your friendship.)

Made in the USA
Las Vegas, NV
15 September 2021